FORTRESS • 95

OTTOMAN FORTIFICATIONS 1300–1710

DAVID NICOLLE

ILLUSTRATED BY ADAM HOOK

Series editor Marcus Cowper

First published in 2010 by Osprey Publishing
Midland House, West Way, Botley, Oxford OX2 0PH, UK
44-02 23rd St, Suite 219, Long Island City, NY 11101, USA
E-mail: info@ospreypublishing.com

ISBN: 978 184603 503 6
E-book ISBN: 978 1 84908 280 8

Editorial by Ilios Publishing Ltd, Oxford, UK (www.iliospublishing.com)
Cartography: Map Studio, Romsey, UK
Page layout by Ken Vail Graphic Design, Cambridge, UK (kvgd.com)
Typeset in Myriad and Sabon
Indexed by Alan Thatcher
Originated by PDQ Media, UK
Printed in China through Bookbuilders

10 11 12 13 14 10 9 8 7 6 5 4 3 2 1

A CIP catalogue record for this book is available from the British Library.

DEDICATION

For Machiel Kiel, in thanks and admiration.

ARTIST'S NOTE

Readers may care to note that the original paintings from which the colour plates in this book were prepared are available for private sale. All reproduction copyright whatsoever is retained by the Publishers. All enquiries should be addressed to:

Scorpio Gallery, PO Box 475, Hailsham, East Sussex BN27 2SL, UK

The Publishers regret that they can enter into no correspondence upon this matter.

THE FORTRESS STUDY GROUP (FSG)

The object of the FSG is to advance the education of the public in the study of all aspects of fortifications and their armaments, especially works constructed to mount or resist artillery. The FSG holds an annual conference in September over a long weekend with visits and evening lectures, an annual tour abroad lasting about eight days, and an annual Members' Day.

The FSG journal *FORT* is published annually, and its newsletter *Casemate* is published three times a year. Membership is international. For further details, please contact:

Email: secretary@fsgfort.com

Website: www.fsgfort.com

THE WOODLAND TRUST

Osprey Publishing are supporting the Woodland Trust, the UK's leading woodland conservation charity, by funding the dedication of trees.

CONTENTS

OTTOMAN FORTIFICATIONS 1300–1710

INTRODUCTION

> 'Architecture is the most difficult of professions, and he who would practise it must, above all things, be pious.'
>
> Koca Mimar Sinan Ağa, the greatest of Ottoman architects (1499–1588)

Despite such imposing Ottoman fortresses as the Rumeli Hisari, overlooking the Bosphoros north of Istanbul, western historians have generally been dismissive towards Ottoman military architecture. This patronizing attitude was typified by K. Andrews in his otherwise excellent book on castles in southern Greece when he wrote: 'To their fortress plans the Turks seem to have devoted either too little or too much attention. The caprice of Mohammed II, who built Rumeli Hisari on the plan of his own Arabic initial, is matched by the rigid symmetry of the star-shaped defences of Yedi Kule at Constantinople... The studied regularity of the Castle of Morea and Roumeli, New Navarino and Zarnata ... contrast with the expedient and skilful irregularity of the fortresses of the Greeks, Franks, and Venetians, who knew better how to fit their walls to the terrain.'

More recent scholars remain critical, maintaining that the Ottoman contribution to the development of military architecture was limited. They are also correct in noting that the imposing Ottoman fortresses of the mid-15th century were rarely followed up on in later years. More to the point, however, they recognized that the 16th century was a period of almost complete Ottoman domination in the Balkans, central Europe, the Middle East and North Africa. Imposing and expensive fortifications were, therefore, generally not needed.

Circumstances changed, of course, and when the Ottoman Empire was forced onto the defensive in the late 17th and 18th centuries there was another wave of enthusiastic military building. It was this latter period which showed how the Ottoman Empire had fallen behind. Yet even here the impression of inferiority is misleading because the Ottomans had limited interest in the highly sophisticated, supremely mathematical and vastly expensive fortresses which now dominated the ideals, if not necessarily the reality, of Western European military architecture. Nevertheless, the Ottomans were aware of their diminished reputation and even the great Turkish traveller Evliya Çelebi (1611–82) felt a need to justify Ottoman work: 'People say the Ottomans do not known how to build fortresses, but anyone who has not seen the fortress

ABOVE LEFT
The central tower of a small castle on Güvercin Adasi (Pigeon Island), overlooking the entrance to the harbour of Kuşadasi on the Aegean coast of Turkey. It dates from the 14th century. (Author's photograph)

ABOVE RIGHT
When the Ottomans captured the Byzantine city of Bursa, they took over a strongly fortified citadel, which they maintained in good repair for many centuries. (Author's photograph)

of Szegedin [Szeged] on the frontier of Erlau, the fortress of Bender [Tighina] on the banks of the Dnister, on the frontier of Özü [Oczakow], and this fortress of Avlonya [Vlorë], cannot understand how masterful the Ottoman construction work can be.'

The character of the Ottoman state changed out of all recognition between the early 14th and late 18th centuries. What began as a tribal *emirate* in a frontier zone between the Byzantine Empire and the Islamic world became one of the early modern world's great powers. It then declined to such a degree that, by the time of the Napoleonic Wars, its neighbours were already thinking in terms of dividing the Ottoman carcass.

The Ottoman state emerged in a mountainous region with few fortified towns but numerous smaller strongpoints, mostly held by Byzantine *akritai* frontier warriors. As support from the central Byzantine government failed, so these outposts fell to the Turks, often when the local lord simply switched from being a Byzantine *akritai* to being an Ottoman *uc begleri* (frontier governor). Under such circumstances the Ottoman *emir*, who was still more of a tribal leader than a ruler of territory, had little reason to encourage castle building. As the Ottoman state grew from a frontier nuisance to a mortal threat, the declining Byzantine Empire and Christian powers in the Balkans put considerable effort into upgrading their defences. All, of course, eventually fell to the Ottomans who thus inherited several magnificent fortifications.

Meanwhile, Ottoman attitudes to fortification were changing. This was already apparent to the great Moroccan traveller Ibn Battuta, who visited the Ottoman capital of Bursa in the 1330s:

> This sultan [the Ottoman ruler Orhan, 1324–60] is the greatest of the kings of the Turkmens and the richest in wealth, land and military forces. Of fortresses he possesses nearly a hundred, and for most of his time he is continually engaged in making the round of them, staying in each fortress for some days to put it into good order and examine its condition. It is said that he has never stayed for a whole month in any one town.

The Genoese were meanwhile concerned for their trading outposts around the Aegean and Black Seas. The Italian humanist scholar Cyriacus of Ancona was usually preoccupied with ancient Greek ruins, but even he noted the strengthening of the autonomous Genoese colony at Galata, facing Constantinople across the Golden Horn. In a letter home, dated late August 1446, Cyriacus wrote:

The Ottoman Empire (frontiers *c*.1609)

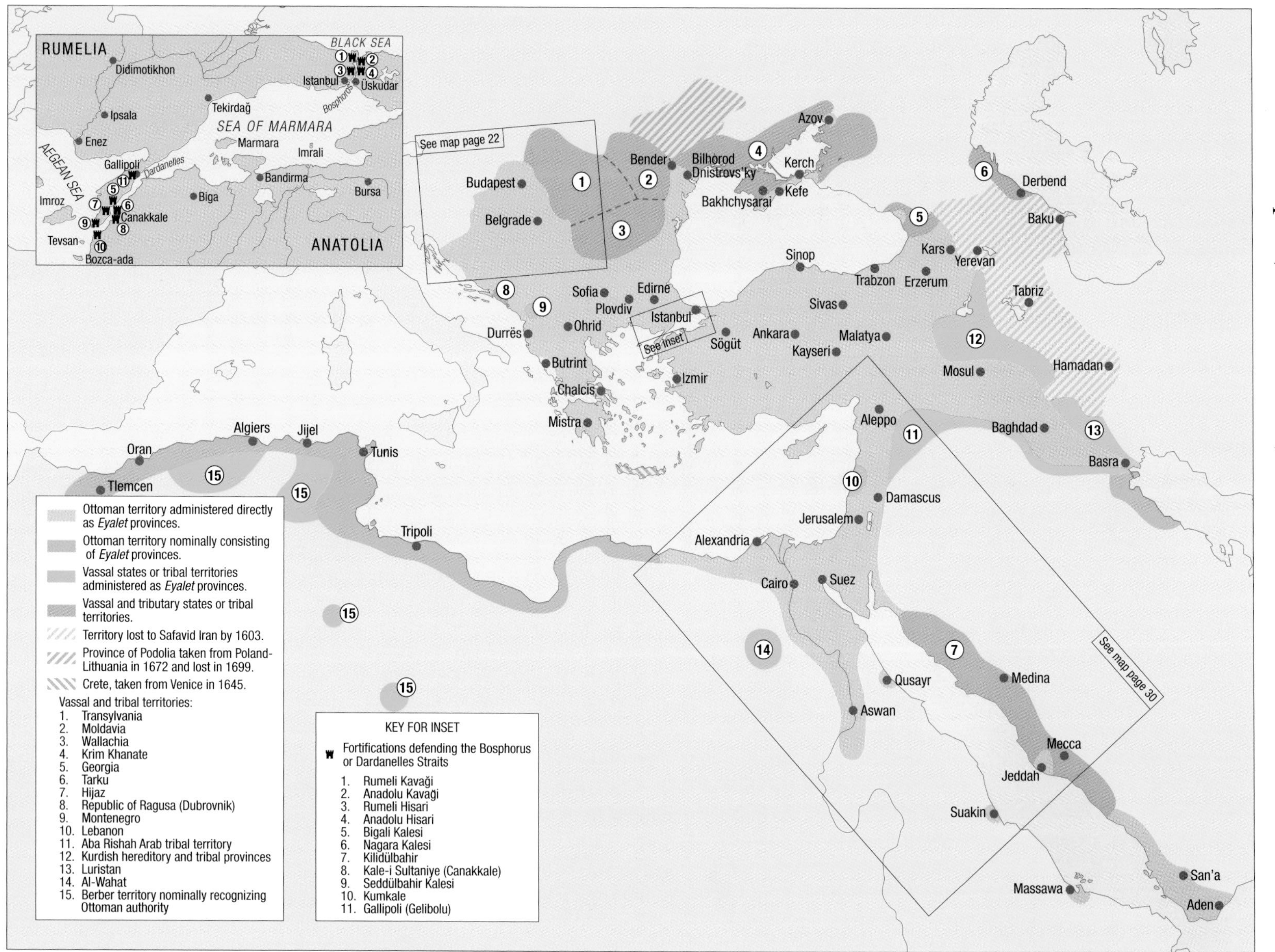

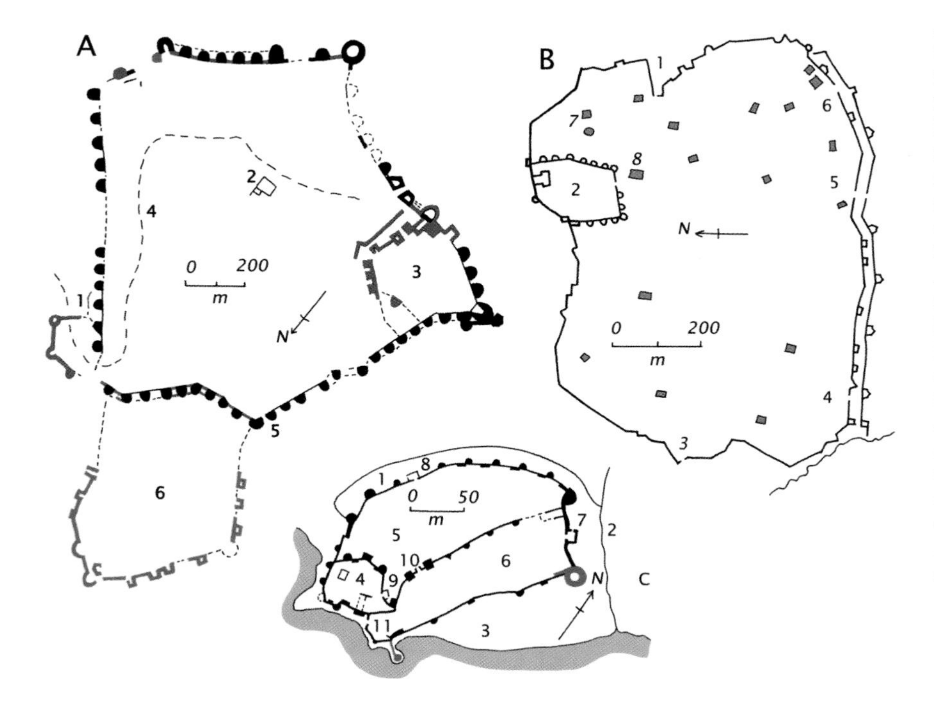

A: Kütahya (after Foss), Byzantine fortifications in black, Germiyan repairs and additions in blue, Ottoman repairs and lower city wall in red: **(1)** lower gate; **(2)** main mosque; **(3)** citadel; **(4)** main entrance path; **(5)** postern gate; **(6)** walled lower town. **B**: Bursa (after Turkish Antiquities Authorities), main Islamic religious buildings in grey: **(1)** Salatanat Kapi (Sultan's Gate); **(2)** citadel; **(3)** Kaplica Kapi (Gate of the Hot Springs); **(4)** Zindan Kapi (Prison Gate); **(5)** Fetih Kapi (Conqueror's Gate); **(6)** Yer Kapi (Ground or Low Gate); **(7)** Tombs of Ottoman rulers; Osman and Orhan Gazi; **(8)** Sehadet Mosque. **C**: Anamur (after Fedden), Karamanid coastal castle with probable Ottoman additions in red: **(1)** moat; **(2)** stream; **(3)** beach; **(4)** inner citadel; **(5)** landward enclosure; **(6)** seaward enclosure; **(7)** main or sea entrance; **(8)** land gate; **(9)** gate of the citadel; **(10)** gate between two outer enclosures; **(11)** postern gate.

On my frequent return visits to Galata aboard our Anconitan and your [Genoese] ships, both on business and out of a craving to go and look at the world, I have watched her with joyful, enthusiastic attention as she has grown day by day in fame and striking ornamentation. For instance, just a year ago, when Boruele Grimaldi was podestà [Genoese governor], in the difficult time of the [unsuccessful] Turkish siege, we saw a tower under the patronage of the archangel Michael had been erected and dedicated to bolster the fortification walls. And in the same vein, when recently, on the 14th of June, I found that you, Maruffo ... by extending the sea wall from the harbour to the Tower of Christ and bringing it to double its original height, you are raising the city daily to greater safety, size and beauty.

Cyriacus himself wrote the text of a marble inscription for these walls, dedicated and presumably paid for by the Genoese inhabitants of Galata, but only seven years later Constantinople fell to the Ottomans, and Galata surrendered without a fight.

DESIGN AND DEVELOPMENT

When the Ottomans took control of the Byzantine city of Bursa they resettled the largely Greek-speaking Christian population further down the mountain, outside the existing fortifications. Meanwhile, the Ottoman ruling elite moved into the old citadel, though quite when the vulnerable Pinarbaşi sector of Bursa was given a double wall is unclear. When the Ottomans reached the coast, however, they faced a different military problem because Christian fleets still controlled the seas. In the Gulf of Izmit, for example, a trusted commander named Qara Mürsel was put in command in 1337 and almost certainly used existing ex-Byzantine coastal fortifications against Byzantine naval raids.

Within a few decades of Gallipoli's fall to the Ottomans, its new inner harbour was fortified with a tower and bridge. (Author's photograph)

The situation was clearer in the second half of the 14th century, when the Ottomans began expanding into the Balkans. Fortifications played a major role from the very start of this process, the Byzantine Emperor John VI giving his Ottoman allies the small fort of Çimbi (Tzympe) as their first foothold in Europe around 1352. Two years later an earthquake caused widespread damage to other Byzantine fortifications in this area, enabling the Ottomans to seize the much more important Byzantine fortress and harbour of Gallipoli. After being lost to a crusade for several years, Gallipoli returned to Ottoman control for good and under the rule of Murad I (1360–89) it became the first Ottoman naval base.

Troops being transferred between the Ottoman state's Asian and European provinces remained vulnerable, so Murad's successor, Bayezid I, had a fortified inner harbour constructed. The Ottomans nevertheless remained a very minor naval power and in 1416 a Venetian fleet defeated their fleet outside Gallipoli. The Venetians attempted to attack Gallipoli's inner harbour 13 years later, but failed to break in. Bayezid I's naval fortifications had proved their worth, yet it was not until the Ottomans won complete control over the Dardanelles, the Bosphoros and the great city of Istanbul (Constantinople) itself that they could ensure their own freedom of navigation in the straits. Even then the Christian maritime threat remained, and thus the defences of the two straits continued to be strengthened.

Whereas the fortifications of Gallipoli were primarily to defend Ottoman communications, Bayezid I built Anadolu Hisari in preparation for a full-scale Ottoman assault upon the Byzantine capital of Constantinople in 1395. It stood at the narrowest part of the Bosphoros, next to the Göksu creek, but given the limitations of existing artillery, was not intended to 'close' the strait. Instead Anadolu Hisari was an observation point and secure position from which small numbers of Ottoman troops could cross the strait and maintain communications with Ottoman forces operating on the European side. Though still a simple fortification, its entrance was designed so that if an enemy broke through the outer defences he could only enter the keep by a flight of stairs that exposed him to defensive fire in the form of a bent or angled entrance of the type known as a *bashura* in medieval times. As part of his more successful effort to close the Bosphoros to enemy shipping, Mehmet II

'The Conqueror' strengthened Anadolu Hisari with an additional three watchtowers. Called the Güzelse Hisar (beautiful castle) in old Ottoman documents, it remains the oldest Turkish (as distinct from Roman or Byzantine) building in the metropolis of Istanbul.

During the second half of the 14th century the Ottomans demolished many existing fortifications in the Balkan provinces of their fast expanding Empire, notably at Edirne, Plovdiv and Sofia. Elsewhere they strengthened existing fortifications, especially along their Danube flank at Silistria, Nikopol and Vidin. The identities of those who built early Ottoman fortifications are virtually unknown, yet their work indicates that they came from a variety of backgrounds. One of the few historians of Ottoman architecture who has 'hands on' experience of the building trade is Machiel Kiel. This has enabled him to dispute the widespread idea that virtually the entire pre-Turkish population in some parts of western Anatolia disappeared during the late 13th- and early 14th-century Turkish conquest. Kiel writes:

Although Anadolu Hisari has been considerably altered, much of the original central keep survives. In the corner between the round tower and wall is what appears to be the outlet from a latrine. (Author's photograph)

> The masonry technique we see in the Turkish structures in Western Anatolia could not have come from the old Seljuk interior of Anatolia. There is massive ashlar work, totally different. My own 18 years as master builder and stone cutter have made this perfectly clear to me, but not to art historians with their academic training, remote from any practical experience. Thus, in short; there was far more continuity between the population of the late-Byzantine and the succeeding Emirate period than was previously supposed.

Although the Ottomans used existing fortifications it was from Islamic traditions of military architecture that they drew most inspiration, most notably adopting the *burj* or large tower as the major element. To this the Ottomans added emplacements for defensive cannon and much thicker walls as a protection against enemy guns, perhaps having learned much from Genoese coastal fortifications such as the Galata Tower overlooking the Golden Horn in Istanbul.

Such 'great towers' formed the basis of Mehmet II's fortress of Rumeli Hisari on the European shore of the Bosphoros, and indeed the Ottoman chronicler Tursun Beg maintained that the circular plan of two of these were in a *firengi* or European style whereas the sole polygonal tower was 'not *firengi*'. Contrary to a myth that Mehmet based the plan of Rumeli Hisari upon his own initial in Perso-Arabic script, the shape of this fortress was determined by the lie of the land and was designed by an architect named Müslihiddin. The remarkable speed of construction – four months and 16 days – depended upon considerable use of prefabricated elements. Partially prepared masonry was brought from Anatolia while ready-hewn timber came from forests along the Black Sea. Other masonry was taken from abandoned local

A Anadolu Hisari

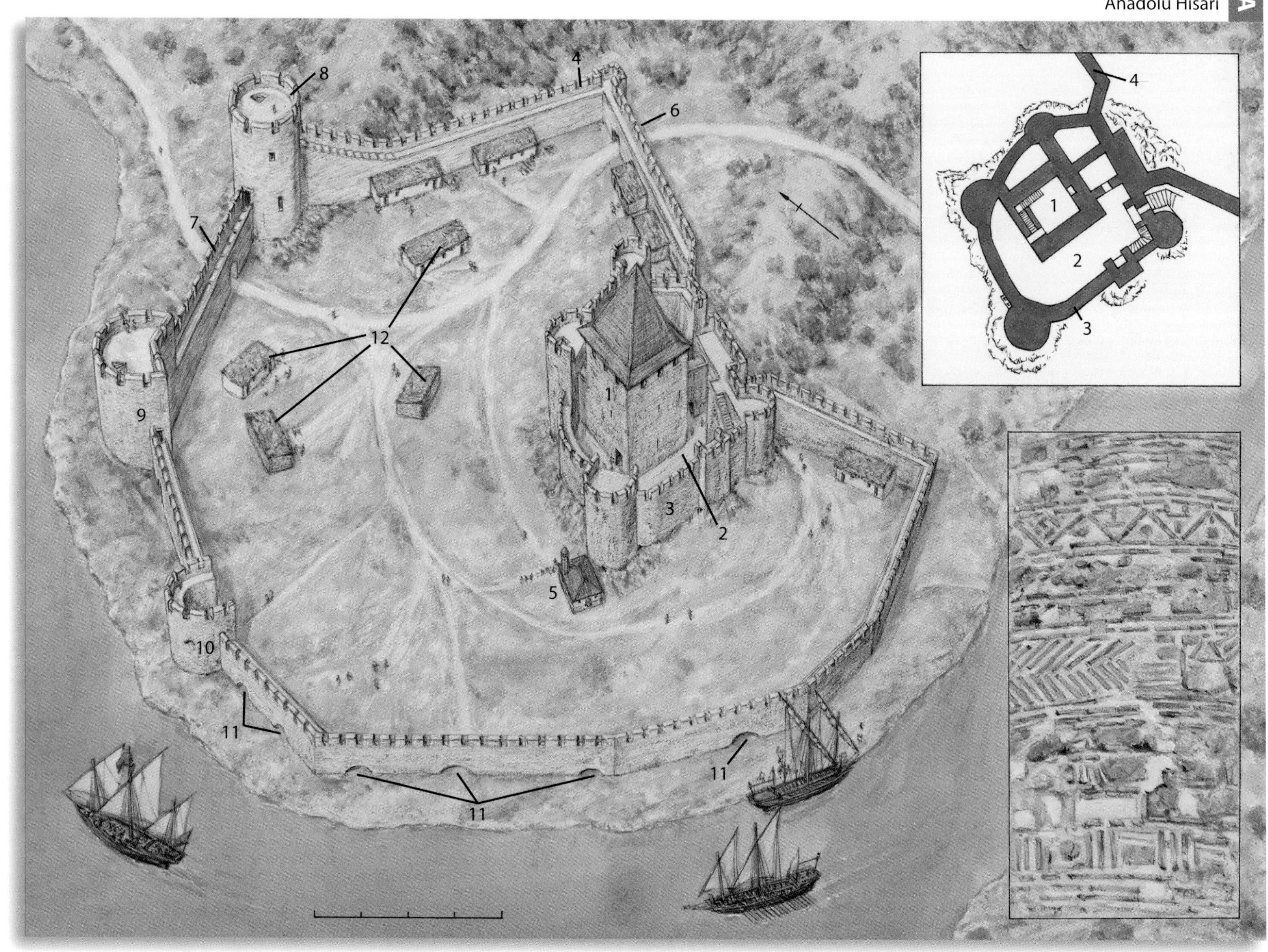

The huge Rumeli Hisari fortress dominated the Bosphoros straits north of Istanbul. Its primary purpose was to house and defend cannon that could close the waterway to enemy shipping, while the fortress itself protected this artillery. (Author's photograph)

churches, the columns of which were then used as bonding agents. Meanwhile, four furnaces to make cement were established across the strait at Çubuklu where woods provided plenty of fuel.

Sultan Mehmet II was just as concerned to 'lock' the Dardanelles; the result being a pair of fortresses built in 1452 at the narrowest point. Though the Kale-i Sultaniye on the Asian side and Kilidülbahir on the European shore were very different from each other, both had 30 cannon, which enabled them to cover the 1,250m-wide Dardanelles. In 1551 both were strengthened by Sultan Süleyman 'The Great' and were again overhauled by Sultan Selim III during the Napoleonic Wars.

The low, almost squat design of the Kale-i Sultaniye reflected its location on relatively unstable alluvial soil next to the river Sariçay. The simple rectangular 100 × 150m plan consisted of outer walls 11m high, up to 8m thick, with nine small bastions at the corners and salient angles between. An inner keep measured 42 × 48m with walls 25m high and 9.5m thick. This had three floors, the stone ground floor being 4m above the level of the bailey while the upper two levels were of timber. They were reached by wooden stairs and included a living area consisting of ten dormitories. Above the top floor was a slightly sloping fighting terrace. Within the fortress courtyard a domed, circular

A ANADOLU HISARI

The small castle of Anadolu Hisari, built for Sultan Bayezid I between 1390 and 1395, was not capable of closing the strait to enemy shipping. Instead, its primary function was to secure the Asian side of a major crossing point, the Bosphoros being at its narrowest here, and to dominate the mouth of a small river which could serve as a harbour. A little over 50 years later, Sultan Mehmet I surrounded Beyazid's simple castle with a curtain wall and towers. Written evidence also indicates that most other structures within the curtain were of very simple construction though the mosque added by Mehmet II might have been more substantial. The inset picture shows some of the decorative brick or tile-work at Anadolu Hisari.

Key to main picture:

1 Central keep.
2 Inner court.
3 Inner enceinte.
4 Outer enceinte.
5 Mosque.
6 Western gate.
7 Northern gate.
8 North tower.
9 Northwestern tower.
10 Western tower.
11 Artillery embrasures.
12 Barracks, stables and storage rooms built of mudbrick with turf roofs.

The oldest illustration of Rumeli Hisari was made by an unknown Venetian artist within a year of its construction in 1453, based upon verbal descriptions by Italian sailors or merchants. (Milan, Biblioteca Trivulziana)

building served as a gunpowder store. A mosque, attached to the main entrance, was built at the same time as the fortress. The ground floor consisted of two domestic rooms while the upstairs served as the prayer hall. While the minaret was plain brick, the keystone of the entrance arch consisted of black and white marble, recalling medieval Syrian *ablaq* decorative masonry.

The Kilidülbahir or 'Key of the Sea' fortress on the Gallipoli peninsula is very different, its original curtain wall consisting of three almost-circular bastions, giving the castle a trefoil plan. Inside, the tall triangular keep has slightly curving walls and is reached by three stone bridges from the outer wall. It was designed with the threat of naval gunfire in mind and it can also be seen as offensive rather than defensive in nature, especially considering its emplacements for anti-ship artillery. Subsequently, the Kilidülbahir was extended under the guidance of French officers during the 18th century.

Once Ottoman rule had been consolidated across the Balkans in the 16th century, relatively few new fortifications were added, at least inland. External threats led to fortresses around the coast and only in a few mountainous regions did bandits continue to defy Ottoman authority. Elsewhere, Ottoman garrisons occasionally repaired Byzantine fortifications in a crude manner. Some fortifications inherited by the Ottomans were of Crusader or Venetian origin rather than Byzantine. For example, the Euripos Bridge from the mainland to Evvoia was already strongly fortified when the Ottomans conquered the island in 1470. Probably built by the Byzantines, then strongly fortified by the Venetians, the Ottomans considered this remarkable structure important enough to maintain until the 19th century.

A good example of the Ottoman focus on coastal fortification in Greece is the fortress of Aya Mavra on the island of Levkas. Here, the collapse of the Crusader rule in 1479 coincided with a major spread in the use of cannon as both offensive and defensive siege weapons. This led to the modification of fortresses almost everywhere, and on Levkas the Ottomans changed the Crusader castle into a modern citadel, surrounding the castle with lower, battered walls about 3m thick. A strong semi-circular rampart, constructed north of the two existing square towers, was given gun emplacements dominating the sea approaches to the town. This new horseshoe-shaped Ottoman citadel covered 5,500m^2 and was further protected by a narrow and shallow moat, the main gate also being relocated in the southwest where it was defended by a two-storey *rondella* (circular) tower.

The strategic situation was different further north, where the Ottomans faced the Kingdom of Hungary. Here, the river Danube was the strategic key, with its Derdap Gorge forming a barrier between the Lower Danube Plain downriver and the Great Hungarian Plain upriver. The northern entrance to this gorge was defended by the fortress of Golubac, which was upgraded during the first half of the 15th century when the Ottomans were already poised at the southern entrance of the Derdap Gorge. Golubac now had an outer ward and a partially fortified river harbour, though the defences themselves were still in a pre-gunpowder style. In the mid-15th century the rectangular towers of its curtain wall were given an additional layer of masonry designed to deflect gunfire, this probably being done when the rump of Serbia was already under Ottoman suzerainty. However, a polygonal gun-tower defending the river harbour dates from 1480, by which time an Ottoman garrison was in residence.

The Ottomans' strategic situation in Albania was again different. Here the turbulent and still almost tribal character of the country meant that most 15th- and 16th-century Ottoman building work was military. One of the resulting fortresses was at Bashtove. Though its earliest phase might include Venetian work, it is more likely that Bashtove was entirely Ottoman, and first built between 1467 and 1479. Being in a flat valley, the fortress is a simple rectangle, measuring 90 × 60m, with towers at each corner and in the middle of three sides. The tower in the western wall was added later, following flood damage. Whereas the corner towers had five storeys divided by wooden floors, the wall towers had only three. All were covered by wooden roofs and had cannon embrasures at ground level. Again in characteristic late-Byzantine and Ottoman style, the interiors of the 9m-high curtain walls were

ABOVE LEFT
The interior of the central tower or keep of the Kilidülbahir fortress, on the European shore of the Dardanelles, shows its unusual 'three petals' shape. Each curved segment of wall was pierced by a gun embrasure so that each floor could house six cannon. (Author's photograph)

ABOVE RIGHT
Like many fortified monasteries on Mount Athos in northern Greece, Stavronikita has a tall tower at the heart of its defences. It dates from the 16th century, when the monasteries on Mount Athos formed an autonomous enclave under the protection of the Ottoman Sultan. (M. Skiadaresis & N. Kontos photograph)

The fortress of Golubac now has its foundations in the end of a man-made lake, which now fills the river Danube's Derdap Gorge. It fell to the Ottomans in 1458, after which the conquerors added the polygonal artillery bastion in the centre of this picture. (Author's photograph)

strengthened by a series of blind arches. These supported a walkway and also had two rows of loopholes separated by a wooden platform. Finally, there was a small *musalah* prayer hall for the garrison above the main northwestern entrance.

Whereas Bashtove was never very important, the fortress rebuilt by Mehmet II at Elbasan was. It was described by the Ottoman traveller Evliya Çelebi in the 17th century:

> This square and solidly built, ancient construction is situated in a broad valley on the banks of the Shkumbin river. It is 15 ells [approximately 6m] high. The outer ramparts of the fortress are skilfully constructed and have 50 towers [in reality only 26]. It is surrounded on all sides by a moat the depth of which is equal to the height of two men. It is 50 ells [approximately 20m] wide and filled with gardens and vineyards. The circumpherence of the fortress is 2,400 paces. It has three iron gates, one to the east, one to the west, and one to the south in the direction of Mecca, across from the coffee houses in the bazaar. This gate is much used and has double doorways, as do the others. The fortress itself has double walls and this is why the gates have double doorways.

However, Vlorë, the largest Ottoman fortress in Albania, seems to have been old-fashioned even when first built, with no defences against cannon, no batter to its walls and no angled or pointed bastions. It protected a magnificent natural harbour and consisted of a huge octagon with eight polygonal corner bastions plus two rectangular towers on each length of curtain wall, one of which served as an entrance tower. Another separate and massive tower stood within the castle, slightly offset to one side. Once thought to have been

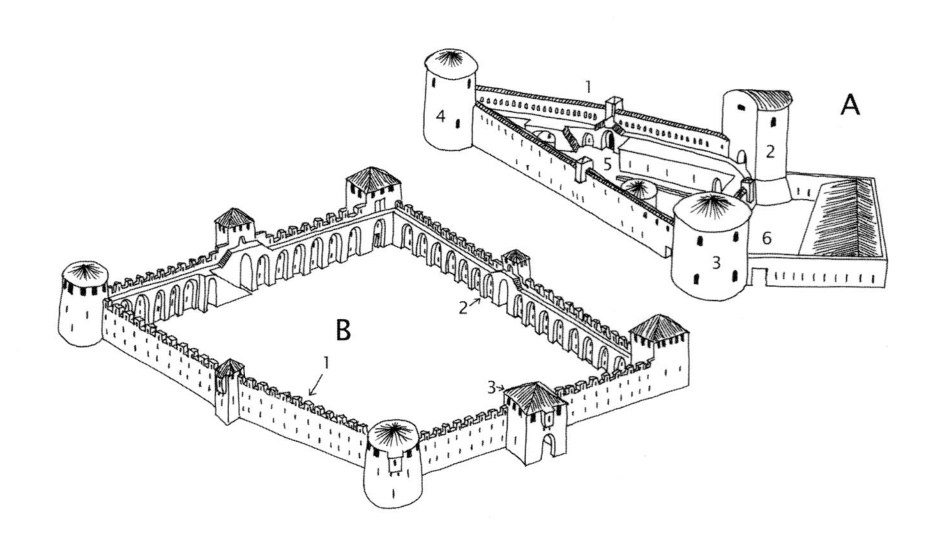

A: Reconstruction of the Ottoman and Venetian fort at Butrint (after Karaiskaj): **(1)** probably Ottoman 15th century fortified enclosure; **(2)** artillery tower in southwestern corner, Venetian late 15th or early 16th century; **(3 and 4)** Ottoman round towers, mid-17th century; **(5)** Ottoman internal buildings, 17th and 18th century; **(6)** Venetian outer enclosure, early 18th century.
B: Reconstruction of the Ottoman fort at Bashtove (after Karaiskaj): **(1)** original Ottoman fort, probably 1467–79; **(2)** western wall destroyed in river flood and rebuilt in 1762; **(3)** *musalah* prayer room above entrance in main northwestern gate tower.

Venetian or designed by an Italian architect, recently studied Ottoman archives show that it dated from 1537–39 and was designed by the famous architectural bureau headed by Sinan.

Information about early Ottoman fortifications in Anatolia is more limited, though the extensive rebuilding of the castle of Anamur – again strategically located on the coast – is confirmed by an inscription dated 874 AH (1469/70). On a completely different scale, there is evidence that the Ottomans and other Turks were already using wooden fortifications in Anatolia during the 14th and 15th centuries, as they would more famously do in Europe in the 16th and 17th centuries. One of these is mentioned in the poetic epic *Destan of Umur Paşa*, written by Enveri around 1465. He describes a Crusader assault upon Umur's capital of Izmir and refers to a 'guard post' erected in front of a narrow castle gate, noting that 'at its entrance was a palisade of solid wood'. This may, however, have been more like a field fortification.

As the Ottoman state increased in size and sophistication, greater emphasis was placed on urban, palatial and 'mercantile' fortifications. When the Burgundian ambassador Bertrandon de la Broquière visited Bursa in 1433 the city consisted of several settlements divided by deep ravines, but he noted that only one was fortified, this being a 'very beautiful castle on a low mountain which is one of the outcrops of the city'. Another town that had a 'palatial' function was Didimotikhon in Thrace, its Byzantine citadel being strong enough to serve as a secure place for the sultans' treasury without significant changes. In contrast, the bigger Thracian city of Edirne (Adrianople) became the Ottomans' first capital in Europe but rather than repair its damaged Byzantine fortifications, the sultans built a new palace complex nearby. It was unfortified but contained at least one defensive building: the Cihannüma Kasri built by Murat II in the early 15th century. Very little survives, but the Cihannüma Kasri was clearly a large rectangular building containing a smaller structure, just under $14m^2$, the latter having a tall central tower with a polygonal top. The only other fortification in the Ottoman palace complex at Edirne was a feeble outer wall, built for Mehmet II, which was more of a boundary marker than a defence.

The first real fortification that Mehmet II added to his new capital of Istanbul was the Yediküle, attached to the inside of Constantinople's ancient Golden Gate. Situated on the site of the abandoned Church of the Holy Apostles, it was not, in fact, the first additional fortification in this spot. Around 1390, the Byzantine Emperor John VII ordered a major strengthening of the towers of the Golden Gate, and between this gate and the coast, to serve as a 'final refuge'. However, these were supposedly torn down again on the insistence of the Byzantine Emperor's Ottoman suzerain. Sultan Mehmet II did much

Like the Romans, the Ottomans built fine aqueducts, many bringing drinking water to their fortifications. This example supplies the citadel of Kavalla in northern Greece and dates from between 1520 and 1566. (Author's photograph)

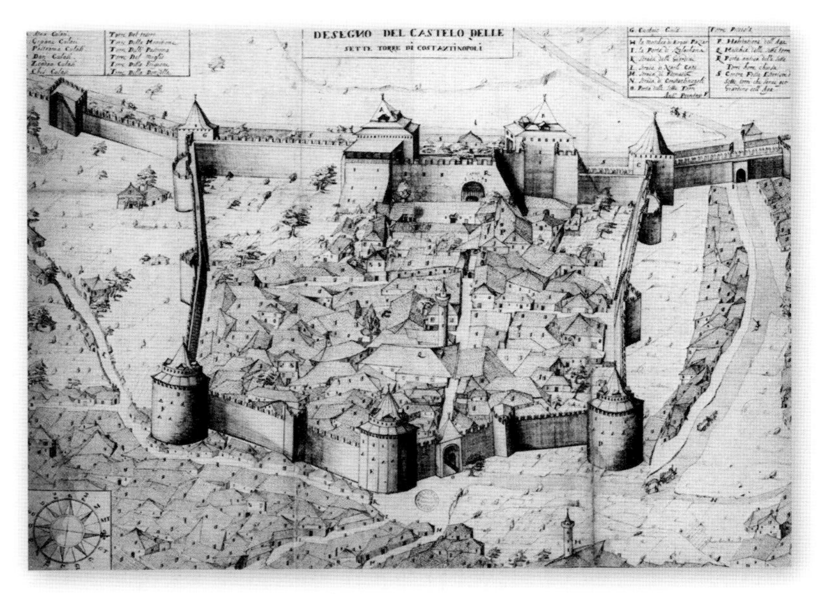

This remarkably detailed bird's-eye view of the Yediküle fortress, attached to the inside of the ancient walls of Istanbul, was made by an Italian artist, probably in the 17th century. The structures and gardens within the walls were for the garrison. (Museo Civico Correr, Venice)

more, adding three new towers to the flanking towers of the Golden Gate and their neighbouring wall towers, linking them with a 12m-high curtain wall to form the Yediküle or 'Castle of Seven Towers'. This was clearly not a defence against external attack, but provided a refuge in case the still overwhelmingly Greek and Christian population either rose in revolt or joined forces with a new crusade. Entry was through a gate on the northeastern side and there was also a small door on the north side, though this was subsequently blocked, while one of the arches of the Golden Gate, though greatly reduced in size, could also be opened. Two of Mehmet's new main towers were circular while the easternmost was polygonal. The design of the rampart walk also provided free movement along the tops of the walls plus access to the towers at the same level.

The degree of security within the Ottoman state almost certainly accounted for the fact that new *hans* or 'secure inns' along its trade roads were generally less fortified than those of previous periods. Other *hans* were located in towns where they became centres of craft manufacture. In almost all cases their defences, insofar as they existed, were against thieves and rioters rather than brigands or highwaymen.

The lives of several 15th-century Ottoman architects are known, though not in the detail of that of the 16th-century master, Sinan. For example, Haci Ivaz, son of Ahi-Bayezit, built the Green Mosque in Bursa in 1419, and according to his tombstone he was also a military commander, scholar

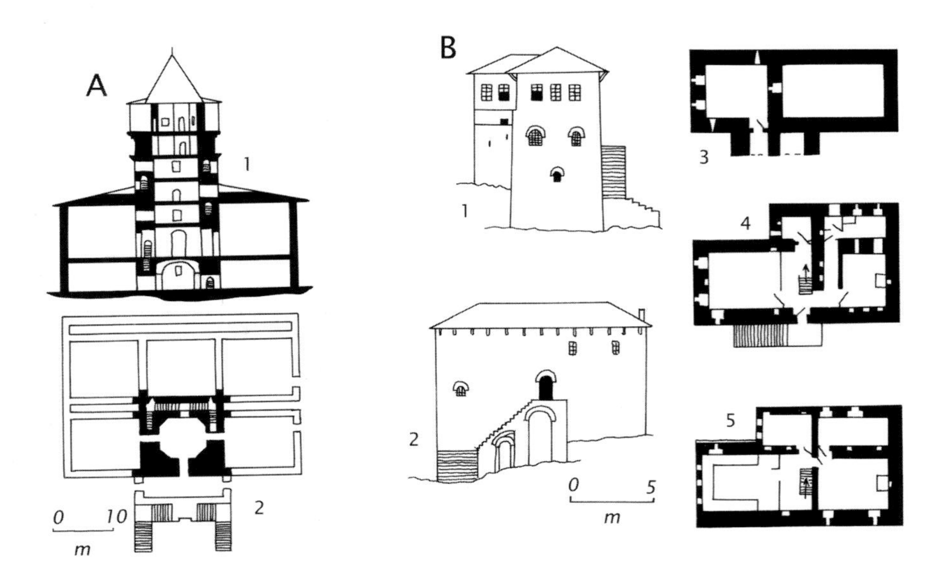

A: Cihannüma Kasri tower, Edirne, built by Murat II, 1404–51 (after Curcic): **(1)** section; **(2)** plan.
B: Fortified house in Girokastër, late 16th or early 17th century (after Lawless); **(1)** side elevation; **(2)** front elevation, **(3)** ground floor; **(4)** first floor; **(5)** second floor.

and mathematician. Whether he designed or built fortifications is unknown, but it seems likely given his military career. The men who did the actual building clearly included soldiers, especially when it came to work on fortifications. According to the late-Byzantine chronicler Kritovoulos, when Mehmet II decided to defend the entrance to the Dardanelles: 'The Sultan immediately sent me to examine the lay of the land and to ascertain the narrowest part and the swiftest current of the strait.' Just under ten years later, after taking Istanbul: 'As quickly as possible he summoned Yakub, Governor of Galipoli and the Chersone, Admiral of the entire fleet and commander of the whole shore, and charged him with the building [presumably meaning the completion] of the forts [of Kale-i Sultaniye and Kilidülbahir], to be carried out as promptly as possible, together with all the responsibility for other things in this connection, without slackening speed.'

One of the three squat, polygonal artillery towers or bastions that the Ottomans added to the late-medieval Serbian fortress of Smederovo at the end of the 15th century. (Author's photograph)

At Smederovo on the Danube, construction of the Ottoman outer walls was apparently done in a hurry by several building crews. Each of the polygonal artillery towers, despite looking similar, are actually constructed using different techniques, with the southeastern tower being very Byzantine in style. This could suggest that the craftsmen came from Skopje in Macedonia, which was already a major centre of Ottoman construction.

The 16th century saw few significant changes in Ottoman military architecture, though it was already becoming old-fashioned compared to that of the Ottomans' European (if not Asian) rivals. Most Ottoman fortifications consisted of simple rectangular garrison fortresses with a remarkable uniformity of design. Their stone walls continued to be tall, unlike the lower, earth-backed walls of more modern European artillery fortresses. On the other hand those that used a mixture of old-fashioned stonework and earth-and-timber *palanka* fortifications were more original and potentially more effective.

The Ottoman Empire was not, of course, just a European power, and fortifications played a major role in its Asian and African provinces. Sultan Selim I (1512–20) conquered huge areas of the Middle East, most notably overthrowing the Mamluk Sultanate of Egypt and Syria, and he is credited with building or repairing many fortresses in eastern Anatolia. Little of his work has been identified, but written sources confirm that the Ottomans began fortifying their Iranian frontier in the 16th century. So it is likely that the largely 15th-century Kurdish castle of Hoşap Kale in the Hakkari province owes something to Selim and his son Süleyman I. It stands on a dramatic crag and has massive towers, the highest of which forms a citadel with seemingly random peepholes made of terracotta pipes pointing in all directions. Perhaps they enabled a sentry to keep watch while sheltering from the fearsome winter winds of eastern Anatolia.

Hoşap Kale stands in southeastern Turkey and is largely of medieval construction. It was strengthened by the Ottoman sultans in the 16th century, and again in 1643 by the local governor, Sari Süleyman Bey. (Author's photograph)

Under Ottoman rule, threats to the security of Syria were different from those seen earlier. Consequently, many of its castles, some of Crusader origin, became redundant. Harim castle may have been typical, remaining little more than a ruin with a few houses for a small Ottoman garrison, whose presence is attested by little more than numerous broken tobacco pipes. Even the Mamluk-era mosque was now used as a workshop. In contrast, nearby Payas on the coast increased in importance, commanding the narrow coastal strip between the sea and the Amanus Mountains. Payas also became a significant port during the 16th century, strongly fortified and equipped with batteries of cannon.

Payas can also be seen as part of a chain of forts along a route from Turkey to the Muslim holy cities of Medina and Mecca. While providing security to Hajj caravans of Muslim pilgrims, these forts and their associated network of roads also served as a military communications system along the Ottomans' desert frontier. Forts deeper within Ottoman territory were stronger and had larger garrisons, while the constant threat of European naval attack from the Indian Ocean also prompted the Ottomans to fortify several eastern coastal cities including Jedda on the Red Sea coast of Arabia, al-Hassa on the Gulf coast and Aden in Yemen.

Egypt, of course, was vulnerable both from the Red Sea and the Mediterranean, which was why several new forts were constructed and old ones repaired during the 16th and 17th centuries. There was even a threat of raiding from the Sudan; the Ottoman Empire marked its southernmost boundary by building the fort of Say on an island in the river Nile near Wadi Halfa. One of the few Ottoman forts in Egypt to have been studied archaeologically is that at Qusayr on the Red Sea. It defended the eastern end of a desert route from the Nile Valley, but as the importance of such routes changed, so their Red Sea terminals fluctuated in importance.

The little fort at Qusayr was originally built in 1571 and consisted of a slightly skewed, four-sided structure with thick projecting corner towers and curtain walls which seem to have been supported for much of their length by stone-walled, barrel-vaulted chambers approximately 4m wide and 6m deep. These might also have provided accommodation and have served as storerooms for consignments of Egyptian wheat that were shipped to the Muslim holy cities in Arabia. Other buildings attached to the interior of the southeastern wall were more complex, perhaps serving as administrative offices and habitation for

LEFT
An Ottoman manuscript 'bird's-eye map' of Naupaktos, known to the Turks as Inebahti and to the Italians as Lepanto, which defended the entrance to the Gulf of Corinth. It was strengthened in 1540, about ten years before this manuscript was made. (Topaki Museum, Istanbul)

the fort's commander. In most respects, however, the fort at Qusayr was similar to other isolated Ottoman military outposts.

The famous White Tower of Thessaloniki is now known to date from Süleyman's II reign, having been built or rebuilt as part of a campaign against Christian naval powers to the west. By commanding the entrance to Thessaloniki bay, it defended lines of communication that might otherwise be exposed to naval attack. The Persian inscription that recorded its construction disappeared shortly after the Ottoman Empire lost Thessaloniki in 1912. However, it had already been photographed by a German scholar and reads:

> At the order of the Lion of the [battle?] field, his Presence
> The Sultan, the Solomon [Süleyman] of his age,
> The Tower of the Lion was made and completed.
> The lion-faced dragon-guns that are on all its sides render
> Lion Tower a suitable name for this tower.
> The date of this tower was 942 since the Hijjra
> Of the Messenger of the End of Time [Muhammad],
> Peace be [upon him].

The Islamic year 942 AH ran from 2 July 1532 until 19 June 1533. Elsewhere in 16th-century Greece, the Ottoman authorities only maintained and strengthened those fortifications that served a vital purpose. In some there was now a clear European or specifically Venetian influence upon their design. In 1573–74, in their new citadel overlooking Navarino Bay, the Ottomans used a modern system of bastions, yet this remained a solitary experiment with no

BELOW
For many years, historians assumed that the White Tower in Thessaloniki was Byzantine or Venetian. In fact it is Ottoman and dates from 942 AH (1535/36). (Author's photograph)

The inner core of the castle at Bilhorod Dnistrovs'ky in the Ukraine is medieval, but after it fell to the Ottomans in 1484 they strengthened its outer defences to resist increasingly powerful gunpowder artillery. (Petro Vlasenko photograph)

known follow-up. Even so, New Navarino was an impressive six-sided fortress, the irregular walls of which followed the contours down to the shore where two strong, self-contained artillery bastions dominated the only practical entrance to the bay and port.

On the other side of the Peleponese lies well-preserved Monemvasia. On top of its great rock stood a citadel, but it is the lower town that is most remarkable. Here the Ottomans added coastal and land walls which ended at the cliff face, though these remain relatively weak, being 2 to 4m thick and from 10 to 20m high with a thin parapet pierced for musketry. While the early 18th-century Rumanian-Ottoman prince and scholar Dimitrie Cantemir described Monemvasia as 'the strongest fortress in all the Morea [southern Greece]', it was the place's naturally strong location that really mattered.

Elsewhere, bastions became more widespread, even if only in simplified forms. From the late 16th century onwards they spread across the autonomous Rumanian principalities, which were, of course, already under strong central-European influence. North of the Black Sea there were several notably strong Ottoman fortresses, mostly sited close to the mouths of the great rivers that flowed from Russia and the Ukraine. At Bilhorod Dnistrovs'ky the existing outer defences are largely Ottoman, consisting of a curtain wall with broad embrasures on top, low rectangular towers and an outer moat. This is similar to the well-preserved Ottoman fortifications at Vidin in Bulgaria and, like the latter fortress, they surrounded an existing late-medieval castle.

Further round the coast, Perekop stood at the entrance to the Crimean peninsula and was the main assembly point for Crimean Tatar forces during the centuries when the Khanate of Krim was a vassal of the Ottoman Empire. The little that is known about its garrison hints at a force of 600 *segban* infantry armed with arquebuses, 20 companies of these men having been recruited from settled villages within the royal domain of Crimean Khans.

The Tatar Krim Khanate, or Crimean Tatars, was the most powerful vassal state within the Ottoman Empire. Nevertheless, the Khan's palace at Bakhchysarai, in the Crimean mountains, was not strongly fortified, though its main entrance had the appearance of a defended gateway. (Mikhael Zhirokhov photograph)

The Ottoman state's most dangerous frontier, however, was in Hungary, facing the Hapsburg Empire. After taking Buda, the western half of the modern Hungarian capital of Budapest, in 1541, the Ottomans established a network of fortifications to defend their extended lines of communication. Those along the middle reaches of the river Danube were especially important. Next came two decades of carefully planned siege warfare, taking and strengthening castles across central Hungary to form a defensible core area, and only after this was completed did the Ottomans focus on a line of frontier fortresses.

While the Ottomans did little to improve existing late-medieval Hungarian fortifications, they now developed their *palanka* system. Timber fortifications had been used in many parts of Europe since ancient times, and the idea that because they are made of wood they could easily be set ablaze is misleading. The timbers of the fortifications, rather than those of the exposed and flimsy internal buildings, were usually massive, often damp and backed by earth. They could not be simply ignited.

Such *palankas* varied in size and sophistication; some lacked any facility for flanking fire while the smallest were little more than wooden palisades surrounded by ditches. Larger *palankas* could be equally simple in design, with a perimeter consisting of a double stockade of tree trunks, the intervening space being filled with earth, resulting in a raised walkway which could be defended by troops or cannon. The timber walls were locked together by a series of transverse logs, which were secured against the inner and outer walls by large wooden pins. *Palanka* walls could be rapidly extended to enlarge a fort's perimeter or to add bastions and other outworks. Though some were attached to important urban centres, most were sited in open countryside near such towns or near smaller settlements. Many were organizationally linked to major fortresses like Varad, which 'possessed' several outlying *palankas*.

Accurate enemy bombardment might take such a system apart, yet this took time and the primary role of *palankas* was to slow an enemy advance, while a more advanced method of construction offered greater security against artillery fire. This was the *horasani palanka*, supposedly named because its colour recalled the dusty pink terrain of Khurasan in eastern Iran. In fact the term probably reflected a very old Turco-Iranian tradition of earth-and-timber field fortifications in which wooden walls were strengthened with pillars of mortar consisting of sifted brick dust and lime. These could only be broken by gunfire at close range.

One of the best descriptions of a fortified Ottoman city in the Balkans came from the pen of the Hapsburg ambassador Ogier Ghiselin de Busbecq, who visited Belgrade in the mid-16th century and, as a professional diplomat, clearly kept his eyes open:

> Belgrade itself lies at the confluence of the Save and Danube, and at the apex of the angle where these streams join, the old city is still standing; it is built in an antiquated style, and fortified with numerous towers and a double wall. On two sides it is washed by the rivers I mentioned, while on the third side, which unites it to the land, it has a citadel of considerable strength, placed on an eminence, consisting of several lofty towers built of squared stone. In front of the city are very large suburbs, built without any regard to order.

One of the most important frontier cities in Ottoman Hungary was Esztergon, the castle of which was substantially rebuilt during their rule. As the centre

Ottoman Frontier Fortifications in Hungary

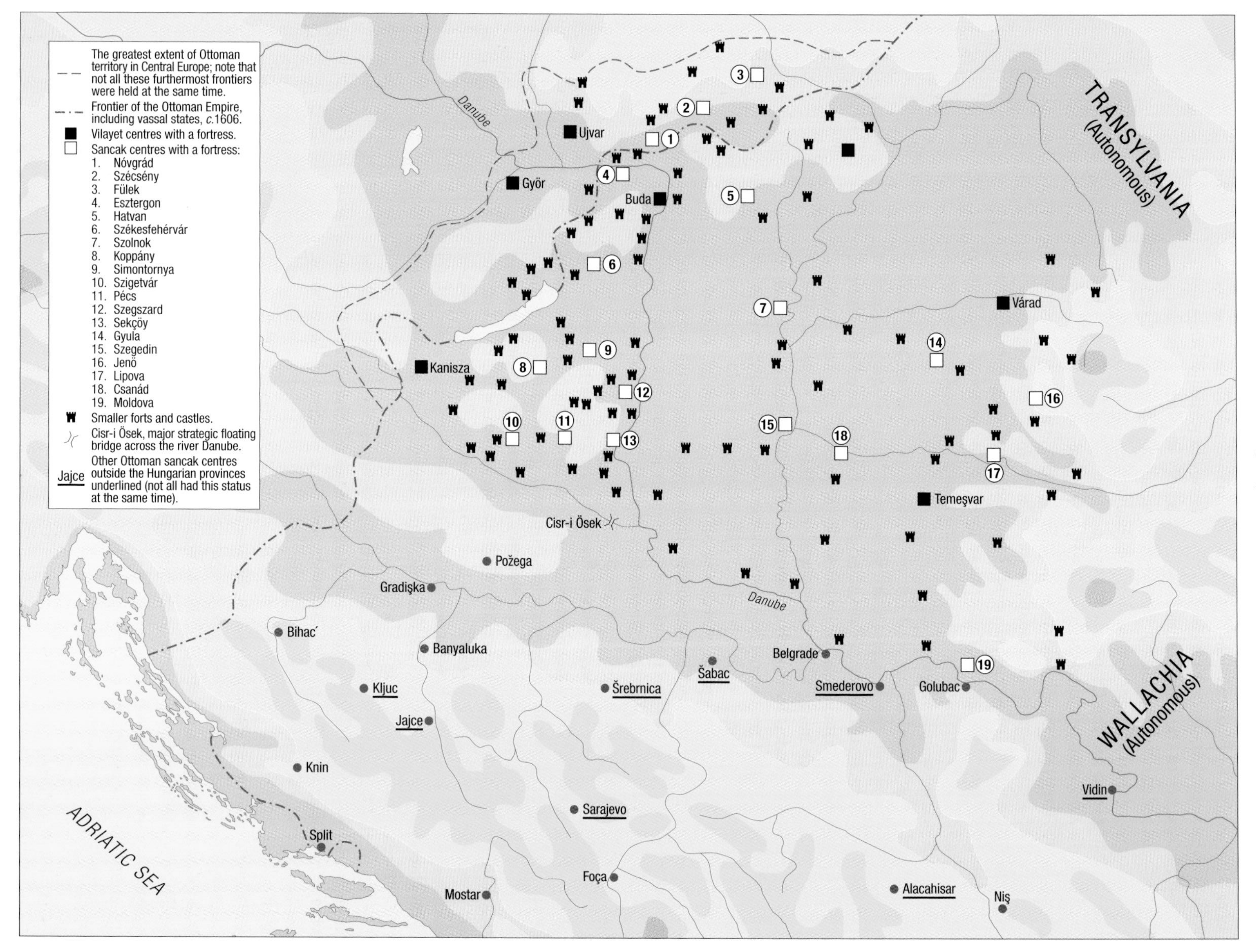

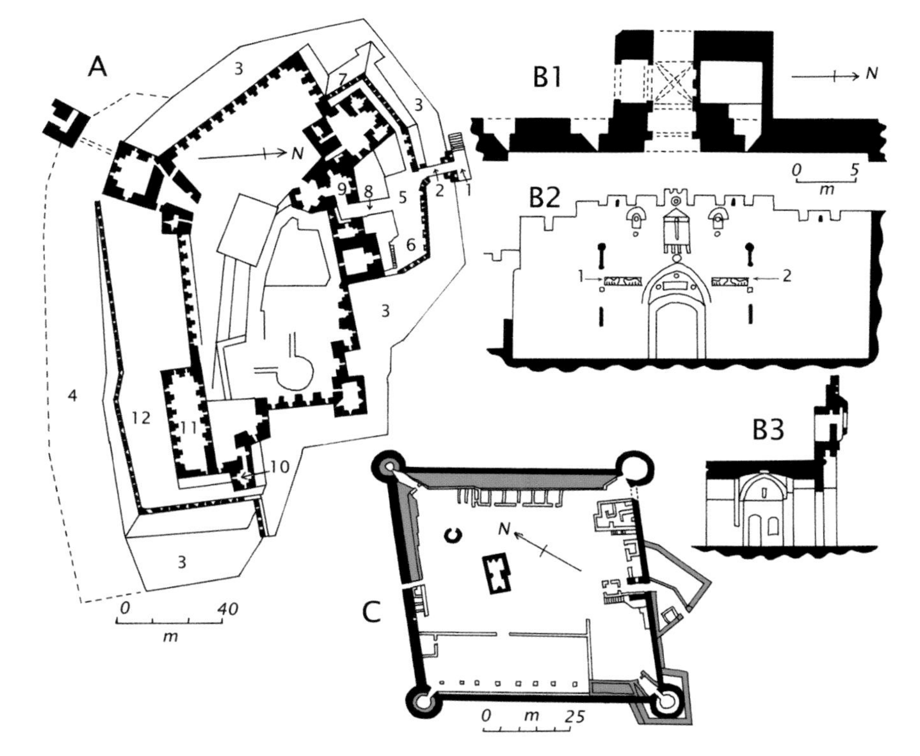

LEFT

A: The main Ottoman restorations and additions to the Mamluk Citadel of Jerusalem (after Hawari): **(1)** entrance ramp and outer gateway; **(2)** drawbridge; **(3)** moat (still existing); **(4)** moat (now buried); **(5)** barbican; **(6)** open-air summer mosque; **(7)** glacis; **(8)** stone bridge; **(9)** entrance passage; **(10)** minaret; **(11)** mosque; **(12)** western terrace of artillery battery.

B: Bab Sitt Maryam (Lion Gate or St Stephen's Gate), Jerusalem, elevation, plan and section (after Hillenbrand): **(1** and **2)** later 13th-century carved panels with the 'Lions of Baybays' inserted in the rebuilt early 16th-century Ottoman gate.

C: Qusayr Fort (after Le Quesne), original 16th-century Ottoman fort in black, late 18th–early 19th-century French additions in blue, 19th- and 20th-century internal structure in outline.

of a strategically important *sanjak* province, it defended the approaches to an important nearby mining area. This was why the Ottomans added modern circular artillery bastions overlooking the wider of two arms of the river Danube, which was a major invasion as well as commercial route.

Perhaps the most famous Ottoman urban fortifications are those of the Old City of Jerusalem. Sultan Süleyman is said to have had a dream telling him to use booty from his campaigns to embellish Mecca and Medina, fortify the Citadel of Jerusalem, embellish the Haram al-Sharif (Temple Mount) and rebuild Jerusalem itself. This story may have come from a 16th-century Jewish writer, Joseph ha-Cohen, who claimed that: 'God aroused the spirit of Suleiman king of Rumelia and Persia and he set out to build the walls of Jerusalem the holy city in the land of Judah. And he sent officials who built the walls and set up its gates as in former times and its towers as in bygone days. And his fame spread throughout the land for he wrought a great deed.'

In reality, the cost of refortifying Jerusalem came from local taxes in Palestine, plus contributions from Damascus and Istanbul. As had been the case in preceding centuries, the Citadel was designed as a separately defensible unit. Here some Crusader work survived though most of the Citadel was of Mamluk construction and even Sultan Süleyman's restoration was quite limited, while an inscription commemorating this work was designed in Mamluk rather than Ottoman style. Perhaps Süleyman wanted to suggest a seamless transfer of power.

Once again the Ottomans' passion for record-keeping means that many details are known. For example, the *sijill* records of the *Shari'a* Islamic court in Jerusalem noted that in mid-September 1531 a curtain

BELOW

The entrance to the Citadel of Jerusalem was built during Sultan Süleyman I's refortification of Jerusalem. Certain aspects of the Citadel's design and decoration suggest that Süleyman wanted to indicate a continuity of authority from Mamluk to Ottoman rule. (Author's photograph)

wall facing the street along the moat had stones missing and the quality of its mortar was poor. City builders who inspected the site found that too much sand had been used and instead recommended using mortar with a higher lime content.

While towers that are known to be 16th-century Ottoman work show that the Ottomans initially built serious and genuine fortifications, many of the ramparts look more like political statements than real defences. As Professor Robert Hillenbrand wrote: 'Thus the upper section of the walls, festooned as they are with bosses, parapets and merlons, are largely for show – hence for example the sudden outcrop of decorative forms in the battlements of the Damascus Gate – though they would assuredly have foiled any attacks by raiding Bedouin. They would have sufficed for small-arms fire, but not for artillery.'

Advances in military technology meant that the great Citadel of Cairo could now be dominated by long-range artillery sited in the nearby Muqattam Hills. During the three centuries of Ottoman rule the relationship between the descendants of the Mamluk military elite who still lived in the city and the Ottoman garrisons who inhabited the Citadel remained tense. Within the Citadel itself more of the existing fortifications are Ottoman than is generally realized. The most obvious new elements are 16th-century defences between the outer and inner baileys consisting of the Burj al-Wastani tower, the Bab al-Qulla gate and the Burj al-Muqattam tower, which is still the tallest structure in the Citadel. Its walls are more than 7m thick and were clearly designed to resist cannon fire.

The military situation in the distant North African provinces was again different. Here the strongest urban fortifications were those of the great port-city of Algiers. At the start of the 16th century its fortified enceinte, flanked by strong bastions, was described by Leo Africanus as 'splendid and extremely strong, constructed of large stones'. According to the French spy Boutin, the towers were 11 to 13m high, with walls 2 to 3m thick, crenellated, with loopholes and 200 embrasures. There was also a fosse, 8 to 10m deep. Outside the city, or perhaps attached to curtain walls, were additional fortresses equipped with a substantial number of bronze cannon to defend the sea approaches.

Most Ottoman fortifications in the harbour area of Algiers have been demolished. However, the Mosque of the Fishers was closely associated with corsair (so-called 'piracy') warfare and was built around 1660. (Author's photograph)

Outside Algiers, a further ring of forts was added at a later date, the most important of which was called the Water Fort. This had 11 embrasures but only ten cannon, whereas the Tamantafoust fort had cannon for each of its 22 embrasures. To the north the 'Fort of the English' defended an entrance to the harbour and had 20 embrasures with cannon. The most famous of the inner ring of towers was the round Burj al-Fanar (Lighthouse Tower) built upon the solid rock of Peñon point. As an autonomous fortification the Burj al-Fanar had its own powder magazine and cistern, was four storeys high, was armed with 55 cannon on two artillery levels and housed a substantial garrison.

Back in the Middle East the Hajj road from Damascus to Medina was moved eastwards to the edge of the desert during the reign of Süleyman I, earlier pilgrims having followed the ancient King's Highway along the eastern edge of the Jordanian highlands. This new route was known as *Tariq al-Bint* (The Daughter's Road), after a daughter of Ottoman Sultan Selim I who had complained about bandits on the old 'King's Highway'. North of Damascus defensible *hans* provided accommodation. South of the Syrian capital pilgrims were expected to camp, each designated halting place having properly maintained wells or cisterns for water. The forts along this route were, in fact, primarily built to protect these water sources and although the earliest specifically Ottoman Hajj forts date from the 16th century, it was not until the 18th century that the majority of such stopping places were fortified.

All Ottoman Hajj forts have essentially the same plan, most being approximately 20 × 20m in their dimensions and constructed of locally available stone. Only in a few places was such masonry finely dressed. Elsewhere a smooth finish was given to important architectural elements by a simple coat of plaster. Most forts were entered through a straight gateway, though those at Muzayrib and Qatrana had bent entrances. Inside, stables and storerooms surrounded a central courtyard, in the middle of which there was normally a cistern or well.

Otherwise the main differences between 16th and 18th century Hajj forts was that those from the earlier period tended to have some decoration such as carved stone rosettes or stone balls above the gate. Other features included stepped crenellations, carved rainspouts and arrow slits with splayed bases.

The Ottoman Hajj fort at Muzayrib in southern Syria is built of the local dark grey, extremely hard, basalt rock, and dates from the early 16th century. (Author's photograph)

B Repairing the *palanka* at Gradişka in 1677

The latter reflect a brief phase in siege warfare when archery and small guns were used at the same time. By the 18th century, arrow slits had been replaced by more numerous but less visible loopholes for musketry.

The towering figure of Sinan dominated 16th-century Ottoman architecture. Other architects are rarely mentioned, especially when a fortification project was of only local importance. For example, the Ottoman chronicler Naima recorded that during a campaign in 1004 AH (1595/96), a gathering of senior officers in the Grand Vizier's tent decided that fortresses were needed to strengthen Ottoman control over the autonomous Rumanian provinces of Wallachia and Moldavia:

> After these matters were fully discussed, it was resolved and agreed to: First, that an impregnable fortress should be built at Bekrish [Bucharest]; and secondly, that a similar one should be erected at the pass of Terghushta [Targovişte]… Once these things were thus settled, the grand vizier and his nobles proceeded to the suburbs of Bekrish and measured off double the space of ground on which Alexandra, the Waiwoda's Monastery stood, and which was formerly a fortress, and made preparations for commencing the first fortress mentioned in the consultation adverted to above. The whole was completed in the place of 12 days after it was fairly commenced.

Given the short time involved, these fortifications must surely have been of the earth-and-timber *palanka* type.

Rather different circumstances led to the repair of a fortified tower in the autonomous Greek Orthodox monastic 'state' of Mount Athos. It is only recorded because the monks needed permission from the Ottoman authorities; this was given in a legal document still kept in the Monastery of Dionysiou. It is dated 20 February 1520 and is an authorization by the *kadi* (Islamic judge) of nearly Thessaloniki, and two *mullas* (Islamic legal scholars) from Sidrekapsi. They testified that the monks Alexios and papa-Maximos asked for permission to repair the tower in front of the door of their monastery because it was ruined and 'detrimental to the monastery'. After personal investigation by the Muslim authorities, the monks' claims were confirmed and permission was granted for the restoration of the tower to its former condition, specified as 15 *kulaç* (approximately 27m) in height and 5½ wide (approximately 9m), with five floors inside the tower.

The 17th century saw widespread modernization of Ottoman fortifications. After decades of relative peace, a new danger

Seddülbahir Kalesi largely dates from the mid-17th century but was almost destroyed by Anglo-French naval bombardment in 1915. This is its shattered southwestern corner tower. (Author's photograph)

B REPAIRING THE *PALANKA* AT GRADIŞKA IN 1677

The town of Gradişka was strategically important because it overlooked a major crossing point over the river Sava. Nothing remains of the earth-and-timber fort, but surviving Ottoman archives include bureaucratic records of its repair in the Islamic year 1088 AH (1677/78). This reconstruction is based upon detailed writings and illustrations by an Italian mercenary named Count Luigi Ferdinando Marsigli. Having been captured by the Ottomans, he accompanied a senior Ottoman officer during the siege of Vienna. The *palanka* therefore consists of an inner artillery fort on an artificial mound, probably of earth taken from the ditch that surrounded the outer palisade. It is made of inner and outer rows of tree trunks thrust into the earth and strengthened laterally by wooden beams and pins. The space between these rows was then filled with earth, though the centre of the emplacement remained open at a lower level. An outer palisade consists of stakes bound together with wattle while the wooden gate has a roofed wooden platform above. Outside, a wooden bridge crosses the ditch.

The simple Ottoman fort at Sigri, on the southwestern coast of the Aegean island of Lesbos, was built in 1747. Its entrance arch was decorated with variously coloured stones, recalling the distinctive *ablaq* masonry of the medieval Islamic Middle East. (Author's photograph)

suddenly loomed from the north in the form of Cossack naval raiders who attacked the Anatolian coast and even ventured into the Bosphoros. To ward off this danger Sultan Murad IV had two new fortresses built, one near the old Byzantine Rumeli Kavaği castle and other near Anadolu Kavaği. Similarly, the Cretan War with Venice (1645–69) not only prompted the Ottoman government to upgrade Kale-i Sultaniye and Kilidülbahir but also to build a pair of entirely new forts at the entrance to the Dardanelles. That on the Asian shore was called Kumkale while Seddülbahir on the tip of the Gallipoli Peninsula is said to have been designed by a European convert to Islam. Though they were too far apart for even the largest 17th-century guns to cover the distance between them, they greatly reduced the area where enemy ships could operate freely.

A new form of artillery fort consisted of circular bastions arrayed like the leaves of a water lily. Known in Europe by its French name of *fleur d'eau*, it was called a *saplija* by the Ottomans because the bastions looked like the 'handles' of a cooking pot. One such *saplija* was built at Foça in response to an attack by the Hospitaller Knights of Malta in 1613. A *saplija* battery was also added to the old Genoese fortress at Mytilene, on the island of Lesbos, probably around 1661. The second gate of the main Orta Kapu Genoese fortress above this *saplija* battery was repaired in 1186 AH (1772/73) but no other major changes seem to have been made by the Ottoman garrison.

By the start of the 17th century the traditional fortifications of Smederovo in Serbia were so outdated that the Ottoman garrison allowed the Hapsburg ambassador Adam Freiherr von Heberstein to study them in 1608/09. He noted that this once-powerful fortress was no longer suitable for modern warfare, its roofs and floors having decayed so much that heavy artillery could now only be placed in the stone towers or on open ground. To the south, in Albania, the Ottomans made use of captured Venetian fortifications such as Butrint. Here, during their late 15th- or early 16th-century occupation the Venetians had built a two-storey artillery tower with loopholes for cannon at the southwestern corner of an existing 15th-century triangular fort. After they recaptured the place the Ottomans added two further gun towers in their

The main fortifications of Lesbos are those of the citadel of the island's main town, Mitilini. Down on the shore the conquerors added this strong artillery bastion, built in a style seen across most of the Ottoman Empire. (Author's photograph)

own traditional style with two storeys, wooden floors and four embrasures for small cannon at first-floor level.

On the Dardanelles, Sultan Selim III had the western wall of the Kale-i Sultaniye in Canakkale largely replaced by modern artillery platforms and ammunition stores, following the designs of a French advisor, Juchereau de St Denys. Deeper inside the strait, the Nağara fortress was only completed after a British naval squadron broke though in 1807, though it eventually consisted of a central citadel shaped like a square upon a circle to which an outer curtain wall was later added.

The original Byzantine northwestern tower of the Yediküle in Istanbul had been rebuilt in 1754/55, but changes to more distant fortifications still tended to be old-fashioned. During their brief occupation of Vidin in the late 17th and early 18th centuries the Hapsburgs began modernizing this strategic fortress, their work then being continued by the Ottomans. Three surviving inscriptions from 1155 AH (1742/43) proclaim the pride of the Ottoman architect, particularly in those defences which faced the river Danube. In Palestine the fortified port of Jaffa was virtually abandoned under Mamluk and early Ottoman rule. It was revived in the late 17th century and became a flourishing port during the second half of the 18th century. Here, recent excavations have identified two distinct phases of Ottoman fortification. The first consisted of a late 18th-century rounded bastion, which was subsequently illustrated by Napoleon's engineers in 1799, while the second phase dated from the early 19th century.

Meanwhile the mid-18th century saw further developments in the great Citadel of Cairo, most notably the construction of an impressive Bab al-Azab (Gate of the Azabs) in 1754. It was built on the orders of Ridwan Katkhuda, commander of the Azab (in Turkish: Azap) troops garrisoning the lower part of the Citadel, who were also traditional rivals of the Janissaries who garrisoned the Citadel's upper enclosure. The gate itself was, however, modelled upon the late 11th-century Fatimid Bab al-Futuh gate of Cairo, perhaps in a gesture of local pride or patriotism. Another powerful figure in Egypt was the governor, Yaksan Paşa, who, in 1786, was responsible

Ottoman Fortifications in Syria and Egypt

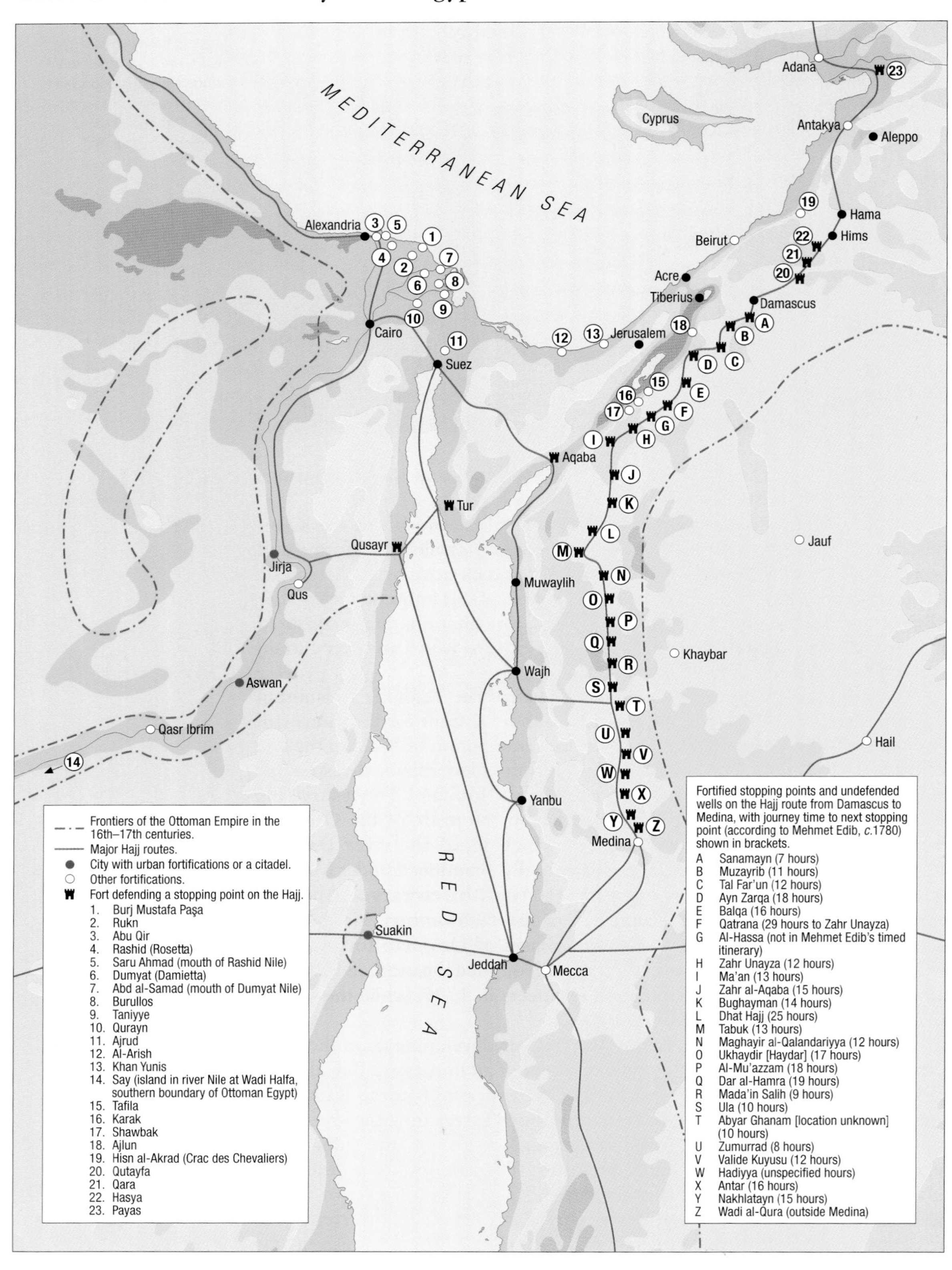

for new walls and a new entrance on the southeastern side of the Citadel, now known as the Bab al-Jabal (Gate of the Mountain).

Other developments in 18th- and early 19th-century Ottoman defensive architecture resulted from political fragmentation and social change, this period witnessing a tendency for local governors to come from powerful families. This, and a widespread decline in local security, led to construction of *konaği*, private palaces or great houses intended to demonstrate the power of such local dynasties. The most famous of these is the castle-palace of Ishak Paşa outside Doğu Beyazit, close to Turkey's frontier with Iran. It is believed to have taken three generations to complete, being finished around 1784, and its design harks back to medieval Seljuk rather than later Ottoman architecture. Perhaps this was another example of growing local patriotism comparable to Ridwan Katkhuda's peculiar Fatimid-style gate in the Citadel of Cairo. The mountaintop *konaği* of Ishak Paşa consists of four courtyards containing separate men's, women's and servants' quarters, a complex of ceremonial chambers, a *hamam* heated bathroom,

TOP
The two fortresses founded by Sultan Mehmet II to protect the Dardanelles in the mid-15th century are shown in this early 18th-century Ottoman manuscript: Kilidülbahir (upper) on the European shore and Kale-i Sultaniye, now better known as Canakkale (lower), on the Asian side. (Museo Civico Correr, Venice)

MIDDLE
This aerial photograph of the Kale-i Sultaniye in Canakkale was taken by a German or Ottoman Turkish aircraft early in World War I, before the fortress was shelled by British and French warships. (Suddeutsche Zeitung photograph)

BOTTOM
The Palestinian town of Tiberius had been fortified during the early medieval and Crusader periods, but these defences were then neglected for centuries. Then in 1738 a virtually independent local Druze leader, Tahir al-Umar, surrounded Tiberius with new but remarkably old-fashioned fortifications. (Author's photograph)

mosque, mausoleum and various other facilities. There were even vineyards attached to the *harem* private quarters. This part of Anatolia is exceptionally cold in winter, so every domestic room has a fireplace while the larger chambers were linked to a central heating system in which warm air passed through earthenware pipes within the walls.

THE LIVING SITES

A substantial number of Turks settled in the Balkans in the wake of the Ottoman conquests, and by the early 16th century Muslims formed a quarter of the entire population, and were especially numerous in Thrace and central Bulgaria. Settlement was, however, concentrated in relatively few areas such as major fortified cities and along important communication routes. The centralized character of the Ottoman Empire also meant that fortresses remained under initially strict government control. As Konstantin Mihailovic, a Balkan Slav soldier who served in the mid-15th century Ottoman army, wrote in his memoirs: '...the Turkish emperor holds securely all the fortresses in all his lands, having garrisoned them with his Janissaries or protégés, not giving a single fortress to any lord: and moreover the emperor holds any fortified city and the fortress within it, having garrisoned it with his own men.'

These fortified places not only guarded the frontier and main routes but also served as administrative centres, while between the larger fortresses were numerous forts, usually *palankas* housing smaller military units. Sometimes, however, local commanders had little control over *palanka* troops, who often behaved more like frontier freebooters. On the other hand, the local knowledge of regional governors was taken seriously on organizational as well as military matters. For example, in the mid-16th century, Kasim Paşa, the *beylerbeyi* (governor-general) of Temeşvar, recommended that if the *beylerbeyi* was based in the frontier fortress of Lipova it would be easier for him to administer frontier districts. The government agreed, and ordered that the *beylerbeyi* and the *bey* of Lipova swap 'bases' while the *mal defterari* (local finance director) also move to Temeşvar.

The overwhelming majority of professional Ottoman troops were Muslim. This is the tomb of Shaikh Muhammad al-Ka'ki, a 16th-century imam of a new mosque built inside the Citadel of Cairo 11 years after the Ottomans conquered Egypt. (Author's photograph)

During this same period, commanders based in Anatolia had similar concerns because their fortifications faced restless local tribes as well as the threat from Safavid Iran. This was made clear in a report by the Hapsburg ambassador De Busbecq, who visited Amasya and wrote:

> The governor of the province is wont to hold his courts, and to keep the main body of his troops... On the highest of the hills which overhang Amasia there is a citadel of respectable strength, which is permanently occupied by the Turks, either to overawe the tribes of Asia, who ... are not over well disposed towards their Turkish masters, or to hold the Persians in check; for, great as the distance is, they have sometimes extended their raids as far as Amasia.

The eastern borderlands of Anatolia nevertheless remained troubled, and the sultans' efforts to impose order were not always successful. In 1551 Iskender Paşa, the governor of Erzerum, seized the fortress of Ardanuç, an important castle in the Artvin area on the border with Georgia, expelling Atabey Keyhusrev II, who had previously supported the Persians. This direct Ottoman occupation worked well for over three decades, but then Sultan Murad III appointed a local Georgian clan called the Poti P'asenc to administer the district, using Ardanuç castle as their base. Unfortunately, they soon became a nuisance to the local inhabitants, resulting in a blood feud that lasted until 1833.

In regions where Ottoman rule was more direct, most garrisons were organized in a standardized way. The Ağa senior commander was normally appointed by central government but they often appointed their own *kethüda yeri* (local lieutenants) from men with local experience. Although Konstantin Mihailovic's memoires were based on his experiences in the Balkans, they are probably relevant for much of the mid-15th century Ottoman Empire: 'The organization in the fortress is as follows: there is one who commands all the others who is called the dyzdar [*dizdar*], like our burgrave [in the Hapsburg Empire]; the second official after him is called the kethaya [*kethüda*] like our steward here; after him are the bulukbasse [*bölük basi*] like decurions amongst us.'

The hilltop fortress of Lipova overlooks the river Mureş in southern Transylvania and was a key military and administrative location for the Ottoman Empire. (Author's photograph)

Qal'at al-Hassa in southern Jordan is a later Ottoman Hajj fort, built between 1757 and 1774. (Author's photograph)

Ottoman records show that the *timars* (fiefs) of garrison commanders could consist of entire villages (*qariye*) or merely part of a village (*hisse*). The smallest *timars* were those held by a *serbölük* commander of a *bölük* unit, while that of a *sertopci* commander of artillerymen was larger. The biggest were, of course, allocated to a *dizdar* fortress commander while that of his *kethüda* deputy was significantly smaller.

Many aspects of the organization of fortresses and their garrisons stemmed from Ottoman methods of conquest during the 14th century. Although many fortifications were demolished at that time, it was also normal for small garrisons to be installed in the remainder, before the main army of conquest advanced further or returned to barracks. Much of the conquered territory was then allocated as *timars* to those of the *sipahi* cavalry who did not already have a suitable fief. Some settled in the conquered villages while others, the *hisar-eri* or *kale-eri*, were stationed in fortresses, where they formed the bulk of garrisons during the 15th century. Here it is worth noting that the majority of *hisar-eri* in the Ottoman Balkans originally came from Anatolia, while most *hisar-eri* in Anatolia came from the Balkans. This was presumably a security measure, intended to inhibit the development of local power groups.

However, a shortage of Muslim military manpower meant that the Ottomans had to recruit local troops from defeated Christian military elites, especially as the Sultans had no wish to see their army tied down in garrison duties. Most remarkable of all was the faithfulness of these local auxiliaries to the new regime, which was a testament to Ottoman tolerance, justice and indeed effectiveness. While such 'native troops' received privileges, usually in the form of tax exemptions, they were still always accompanied by Ottoman regulars. Tax privileges could also be given to entire fortified towns, Muslim and Christian inhabitants included, in return for military and political faithfulness. Konya and Kayseri were exempted 'on account of the faithfulness which they had shown during the wars with Uzun Hasan [Aq Qoyunlu ruler and bitter rival of the Ottomans, 1457–78]'. Similarly, the inhabitants of Croïa in Albania were offered tax exemption in return for guardianship of the fortress shortly before the area was attacked by Skanderbeg, the famous Albanian resistance leader.

During the 16th and 17th centuries, units of specialist troops emerged with a specialized local security role. The most important were the 'fortress guards', the *derbendci* (guardians of passes), and the permanently mobilized 'frontier raiders'. Within fortress garrisons there were also increasingly specialized units whose members received specific rates of pay.

The backbone of the most important garrisons were, of course, Janissaries. Their corps eventually had three elements, the largest being the *Cema'at* (assembly) of 101 *orta* (hearths) whose bases rarely moved from the location where the unit was created. Sometimes called 'fortress Janissaries', they garrisoned the main fortified cities and numbered around 12,000 in 1519, rising to approximately 48,000 in the 1650s. Elsewhere, the numbers of resident Janissaries could be very small. Until the 17th century those living on the Greek island of Lemnos, for example, numbered around 20, while the rest of the 280-strong garrison were local Greek Christians. The Topçu Ocaği (Cannon Corps) and Top Arabaci (Cannon Waggon Corps) had their main barracks in Istanbul but some units were based in the main fortresses while a few specialized units were tied to particular places. Thus the Cema'at-i Cebejiyan-i Kal'a-i Misir (Corps of armourers of the Citadel of Cairo) normally only served in Egyptian fortresses.

Another element were the *gönüllü* 'volunteers', a name given to many in the pay lists of fortresses. They ranged from elite cavalry to servants, 'attendants of castle guards' and *ma'zul* ('dismissed' members of garrisons). Officers' servants who took up arms were listed as *gönüllü*, many in an effort to be accepted into a registered military unit with its increased pay and status. Occasionally men who had been demoted wanted to redeem their reputations and became *gönüllü*. They included Seyfeddin, a former *kethüda* deputy fortress commander in the *sancak* of Semendire, who marched as far as Iran to 'prove with his deeds that he deserved the Sultan's bread'. He succeeded and was assigned a *timar* worth twice what he had before.

Once again the Ottoman passion for keeping records provides remarkable detail about garrisons as far back as the 14th century, when the first Janissary *Cema'at* units probably replaced less reliable and untrained *yaya* in important fortresses. The *yaya* themselves seem to have been recruited from recently settled Turcoman nomads whose lack of discipline made them unsuited to garrison work. Another source of garrison troops were the *azaps*. First recorded as naval marines and light-infantry archers in the early 14th century, by the late 14th century they were serving in fortified locations as pickets, night-time guards or to ensure local tax collection.

The Anatolian Turkish city of Kayseri had been fortified for hundreds of years, but its defences were repaired and strengthened by Sultan Mehmet II in the late 15th century. (Author's photograph)

Extraordinarily detailed information is found in an Ottoman register drawn up 16 years after the conquest of Trabzon on the Black Sea. It shows that although the majority of the resident Christian families remained, the old Byzantine military aristocracy had been expelled from the citadel, largely being replaced by Turkish *azaps*. On the other hand, there was still a Christian community within the fortress of nearby Giresun, responsible not only for its defence but remaining on the naval muster.

Vidin in Bulgaria has been studied in similar detail. During the 15th and early 16th centuries Vidin formed an important part of the *serhad* 'frontier zone' facing autonomous but not necessarily reliable Wallachia and the still-powerful Kingdom of Hungary. As a result, Vidin and the forts of its *sancak* province were strongly garrisoned. Most of the local Muslim men belonged to one of its corps, either *timarli sipahi* cavalry, *mustahfizan* fortress guards or *akinci* raiders. Many local Christians were meanwhile enlisted in paramilitary corps such as the *filurciyan* and the *voynuğan*.

Numbers increased over the years, and during the early part of Süleyman II's reign there are understood to have been 9,653 registered *timar* holders in additional to the regular *sipahi* cavalry. These men served in fortress garrisons, with 6,620 being based in the European provinces and 2,614 in Anatolia, but only 419 in the Arab areas, though this number would soon rise. These figures excluded Janissaries and *azaps* who did not have *timar* fiefs, there being no less than 2,000 Janissaries in Baghdad alone.

Two important but different fortified cities can be taken as examples. In 1529 the unit of *topçus* and *kalafatçis* at Belgrade still included seven Christians, but as the years passed greater numbers of Muslim troops acquired their specialized skills in artillery and explosives. By 1560 the 48 *topçu* artillerymen in Belgrade consisted of 35 Muslim and 13 Christian artillerymen; the proportion of non-Muslims continued to decline thereafter.

Unlike Belgrade, Damascus had been an Islamic city for centuries, though it continued to have substantial and flourishing Christian and Jewish minorities. Here the Janissaries who had arrived during or immediately after the Ottoman conquest in 1516 were rapidly assimilated into the local Syrian population, their descendants being known as *yerli kullari*. The *kapi kullari* were also Janissaries, but they were descended from troops sent from Istanbul in 1658/59. Clashes between these two Janissary *ortas* would disturb Damascus until the 'central government' *kapi kullari* unit was disbanded in the 1740s, so perhaps Aleppo was fortunate in only having one resident *orta*.

Cairo suffered similarly from rivalry between different elements in its garrison. Almost the entire Mamluk leadership had been wiped out during the Ottoman conquest of Egypt but their sons, the *awlad al-nas*, were largely spared. An amnesty was then announced, and after a while the remaining Mamluks were included in the military payroll at a reduced rate. Even so, after the death of Khayrbak, the first Ottoman governor of Cairo, all Mamluks were again expelled from the Citadel. Specifically Ottoman units now took over and remained there until Egypt reasserted its independence in the 19th century. The changeover from a Mamluk to a Janissary and *azap* garrison seems to have been extremely thorough, as recorded by the Egyptian observer Ibn Iyas:

> The [new] viceroy [Mustafa Paşa] took the keys of all the storehouses and hawasil [depots] from the bawwabun [doorkeepers], and handed them over to a group of Arwam [Janissaries] of his own retinue, and drove away all the doormen, servants, troops, jockeys, attendants, and others. He even dismissed the cooks

> of the Royal Kitchen and the water carriers, and replaced all these with Arwam. He also dismissed all the Qur'an readers in the Citadel, as well as all the muezzins, and appointed just one muezzin to the mosque of al-Hawsh [the governor's own palace or residence].

Evliya Çelebi almost always exaggerated the size of Ottoman garrisons in his *Seyahatname* (*Book of Travels*), but accurate information survives in Ottoman government records, usually in the form of payroll lists. These indicate not only numbers but also the types of troops in specific garrisons at specific dates. A good example of a well-established garrison containing a wide variety of troops was that at the town of Kanizsa in Hungary. In 1024 AH (1616/67) it consisted of four *çavus-i divan* NCOs, eight *cebeci* armourers, 19 *segban* infantry, 23 *topçu* artillerymen, 25 *müstahfiz* 'fortress soldiers', 155 *yeniçeri* (Janissaries), 295 *faris* cavalrymen and 19 religious officials. Five years later, when the frontier had calmed down, the same fortress had four *çavuş-i divan*, eight *anbarci* (storekeepers), 22 *cebeci*, 34 *topçu*, 65 *martolos* (Christian auxiliaries), 84 *müstahfiz*, 113 *yeniçeri*, 592 *faris*, 661 *azap* lower-grade infantry, 50 unspecified men and 11 religious officials.

Because Kanizsa was a large town it might be expected to have a larger garrison than the smaller Ujvar, but Ujvar was closer to the frontier and so its troops were usually more numerous, particularly in the late 17th century when they often numbered over 2,000 men. For the same reason there was a higher proportion of Janissaries and *gönüllü* volunteers in Ujvar. In fact, the defensive rather than offensive role of Kanizsa was clear in its larger number of armourers and artillerymen. Sometimes such garrisons were very large indeed; Azov on the exposed northern coast of the Black Sea contained 3,656 troops in the late 17th century, of whom 2,275 were Janissaries. In contrast, Kütahya, in western Anatolia and far from any frontier, was the capital of a very large province. Its citadel garrison, according to an Ottoman document of 1698, consisted of only 119 fortress guards, each armed with two pistols, a musket and assigned a *timar* fief. The castle nevertheless still had a *dizdar* commander who might, in the circumstances, be better regarded as a warden. As usual he received a large income from his *timar*.

During this period it would seem that relatively peaceful regions like Anatolia were militarily more important as sources of recruits for garrison troops who then served elsewhere. Most of the *segban*, whose numbers in Syria increased dramatically by the early 17th century, seem to have come from Anatolia. Under their *bölük başi* unit commanders, their main role was now that of arquebus-armed infantry, cavalry and garrison troops. Most of the *kapi kullari* Janissaries in Syria also came from elsewhere, including Thrace, western Anatolia, Iraq, and from Kurdish tribes. However, the *müstahfiz* Janissaries who garrisoned the Citadel of Cairo in the 16th century seem to have been largely local. In 1674 there was a total of 15,916 soldiers registered in the Citadel, of whom 6,461 were Janissaries while only 2,205 were *azaps*. Their *ağa* was nominated by Istanbul, but real power increasingly lay in the hands of a locally promoted *kethüda* 'lieutenant' who only held his position for one year.

The traditional Ottoman system of garrisons remained largely unchanged through the 18th and into the early 19th century, but its effectiveness was clearly declining. This in turn contributed to a decline in the characteristic tolerance that had been a hallmark of Ottoman civilization. Ottoman territorial losses also meant that Vidin once again found itself in a vulnerable frontier zone and flooded with Muslim refugees. Following a request by the local Janissaries,

C Simnic's Tower, Kratovo, Macedonia, second half of the 14th century

Amongst the complex of Ottoman buildings at Payas, on the Gulf of Iskenderun, is a small but well-built 16th-century fort. (Author's photograph)

all Christians were expelled from the fortified part of Vidin and had to live outside its walls. They were also forbidden to build stone houses, which could be used as strongpoints by potential besiegers. As a result, the fortified old town of Vidin was defended entirely by Janissaries and locally recruited *yerlü* troops. By 1750 there were no less than 5,440 Janissaries in Vidin alone; this was more than any other Balkan city other than the equally threatened Belgrade. On the other hand such figures can be misleading, as many of those registered as Janissaries were at best part-time soldiers who meanwhile also numbered amongst the *beşe* (craftsmen) of Vidin.

The famous Janissary Corps was, of course, now militarily in steep decline. Yet between 1693 and 1722 there were still only 800 to 1,200 'local' Janissaries in Damascus while between 1701 and 1735 the number of 'imperial' Janissaries of Damascus ranged from 268 to 413. Amongst the small numbers of other troops now forming part of the city's garrison were *lawand*, *dalatiyya* and reasonably well-disciplined *tüfenkji* (musketeers) who were mostly

C SIMNIC'S TOWER, KRATOVO, MACEDONIA, SECOND HALF OF THE 14TH CENTURY

The tradition of fortified tower-houses was an old one in the Balkans. Today few survive, but six can still be seen in the Macedonia town of Kratovo. Although some may date from before the Ottoman conquest, the best-preserved, known as Simnic's Tower, includes Turkish or Islamic architectural features and is probably one of the earliest Ottoman fortified buildings in Europe. Like the other domestic towers in Kratovo, the ground floor was probably used as a storeroom while the upper floors were living areas with large windows. The corners of the building, as well as the windows and doors, are made of finely cut masonry, whereas the rest of the structure is made of semi-finished stone. The entrance into Semnic's Tower is on the eastern side, 3.35m from the ground and originally reached by removable wooden stairs.

Key to main drawing:

1 Domed upper chamber.
2 Stucco decoration on the zone of transition between walls and dome.
3 Ottoman-style fireplace with conical hood.
4 Domed roof of second floor supported by blind-arch squinches.
5 Staircase within the external wall.
6 Shallow dome of first floor supported by undecorated squinches.
7 Shallow dome of lower floor on undecorated squinches.
8 Entrance.
9 Wooden staircase from exterior ground level to tower's entrance.

Key to inset drawing:
Plan of the lowest chamber in Simnic's Tower

1 Entrance.
2 Staircase within the thickness of the wall.
3 Small chamber, perhaps for guard to store weapons.

employed in local security. Meanwhile, *maghariba* (westerners) from North Africa often protected Hajj caravans travelling from Damascus to Mecca and Medina.

Local levies were normally only summoned in emergencies and during the 18th century these included men from all the numerous religious sects of Syria. Towards the end of the 18th century there was also a brief revival of the old system of slave-recruited Mamluk soldiers in Syria, Iraq and Egypt. Small numbers of such troops were purchased by various semi-independent local rulers or regional governors. In late 18th-century Cairo, the balance of local military power had shifted dramatically with almost all senior officers now being of Mamluk origin. A few were recently purchased men of Circassian, Georgian, Kurdish, Bosnian and Albanian origin, and even of Anatolian Turkish, Armenian and Jewish origin. These were the Egyptian leaders who would shortly face Napoleon's army at the Battle of the Pyramids.

THE SITES AT WAR

The frontier zones which separated the Ottoman Empire from its European neighbours, and where most of its fortifications were located, had much in common with the frontier zones that had earlier separated the Byzantine Empire from its Islamic neighbours. As a result, Ottoman garrisons, especially those of smaller fortified outposts, continued many of the traditions of their medieval predecessors – the Muslim *gazis* and the Christian *akritai*. In fact, during the early centuries many were recent converts to Islam. In this situation their code of frontier behaviour remained similar to military attitudes of the medieval period.

They took part in major military campaigns but tended to ignore official periods of peace by continuing to raid and be raided. Correspondence between governments complaining about this state of affairs tends to be couched in general terms whereas correspondence between the commanders of fortified outposts provides much more detail. It becomes clear that garrison troops, especially volunteers, were less interested in destroying the enemy than in capturing booty or prisoners. Casualties also tended to be surprisingly few. In the words of Peter Sugar, a historian of southeastern Europe under Ottoman rule: 'A dead peasant could not produce, a dead soldier could not be ransomed, a totally destroyed field could not be worked for years. Life, therefore, became somewhat more valuable on the frontier than it was when regular armies clashed.'

The role of Ottoman fortifications as offensive bases was the same as it had been throughout pre-modern warfare. For example, after Bilhorod-Dnistrovs'ky fell to the Ottomans in 1484, this fortress became a strategic base from which to attack and dominate Moldavia. After that had been achieved, Bilhorod-Dnistrovs'ky contributed to Ottoman 'defence in depth', first against the kingdom of Poland-Lithuania and subsequently against an ascendant Russia.

In fact, the Ottoman Empire maintained several major fortified bases behind each of its most war-torn frontiers. In the east Erzerum faced Iran while Diyarbakir, Van and Mosul faced Iraq. In Europe great rivers marked some frontiers, but more commonly they linked major bases: Azov and Yeni-Kale being on the Don; Ochakov and Kilburun on the Dnepr and Bug; Bilhorod-Dnistrovs'ky, Tighin [Bender], Kamianets Podolsky and Khotin on the Dnister; Kiliya, Ismayil, Tulcea, Braila, Silistria, Ruse [Rusçuk] on the lower Danube and Belgrade on the middle Danube. Where such river communications were

LEFT
Although the Ottomans did not hold Kamianets Podolsky for long in the second half of the 17th century, they clearly intended to make it a formidable frontier outpost. They repaired the medieval bridge, now called the Turkish Bridge, and added a minaret to the Catholic church when they converted it into a mosque. (M. Zhirokhov photograph)

lacking, fortified bases such as Thessaloniki, which was the main base for operations in Greece and Albania, were usually on the coast.

The relationship between galley fleets and their fortified home ports remained central to Ottoman naval warfare. This also extended further afield, with fleets working in strategic and sometimes even tactical cooperation with other coastal or island fortifications. A variation on this theme could be found in the Black Sea where, after its navy had won complete domination, the Ottoman state took care to 'plug' the outlets of the great northern rivers with fortresses or fortified cities. One such was Azov at the mouth of the Don, which had a stone wall, 11 towers, a ditch, an earthen rampart and a garrison of normally 4,000 troops. The Don, of course, came from deep within hostile Russia and the strategic importance of the area was such that it was known as the Seddül-Islam (the 'Dam' or 'Barrier' of Islam).

During earlier centuries, however, the most dramatic role of Ottoman fortifications was to strengthen the blockade of an enemy city. This started during the first half of the 14th century according to traditional Turkish accounts of the sieges of Bursa and Iznik by the *emir* Othman. These mention *havale* forts, one of which was built near Iznik. Its garrison of 100 men was tasked with stopping provisions from entering the city. An account of the Ottoman conquest written by a certain Idris about a century later noted that: 'The tower built by Othman became known as Targay Hisari after one of his brave and trusted men. The ruins of this tower are still visible.'

One of the few 14th-century Turkish literary sources to describe Muslims defending a fortress is a translation by Yusuf-i Meddah of the earlier Persian *Varqa ve Gülşah* epic

BELOW
Two of the pairs of Ottoman fortresses built to prevent enemy fleets penetrating the Dardanelles are shown on this 18th-century French engraving. Kilidülbahir and Kale-i Sultaniye are simply labelled as 'Les Dardanelles'. Towards the bottom of the picture Seddülbahir and Kumkale are indicated as 'Château neuf d'Europe' and 'Château neuf d'Asie' respectively. (Photograph via Canakkale Castle Museum).

poem. Here the 'City of Yemen' comes under siege, and 'within the city the people, the Amir and the Vezir are helpless, captives within the blockade'. Later, 'the city dwellers in the siege, pretend to be soldiers', thinking themselves saved, and 'on top of the rampart they beat [the drum announcing] good news. They revelled in pleasure and joy'. Even here, it seems, the Turkish poet shows his poor opinion of part-time urban militias who defended fortified places.

The Kanli Kule fortress was built by the Ottomans to defend the entrance to the Gulf of Kotor in Montenegro in 1483. It was badly damaged by mining during a Venetian siege almost exactly two centuries later. (Author's photograph)

One of the Ottoman Empire's most important defensive siege operations during the 14th century was at Nikopol (Nicopolis) in northern Bulgaria. Here in 1396 an elite Ottoman garrison held its position against a huge Crusader army, which had already taken two major fortresses and slaughtered their garrisons. Most early accounts of this campaign naturally focus on Sultan Bayezid's great victory outside Nikopol but they also include some facts about the defence of the fortress. For example, a small Ottoman outpost on the opposite bank of the Danube had almost certainly been overrun or withdrawn and although Nikopol stood on a high bluff overlooking the river, it was soon surrounded, with an enemy fleet anchored in the river and a Crusader army encamped outside its walls.

After being incorporated into the Ottoman state, the defences of Nikopol were strengthened or repaired, and a large, well-supplied garrison installed under an experienced officer named Doğan Beg. A direct Crusader assault was beaten back, so the invaders settled down for a prolonged blockade, knowing that the Ottoman garrison would run out of food whereas they were supplied by boat from friendly Wallachian territory north of the Danube. Sultan Bayezid's vanguard then came into view on 24 September, and Bayezid arrived and established camp several kilometres south of Nikopol. Later Ottoman sources also maintain that the Sultan reached the walls of the citadel, probably at night, and spoke to the garrison commander. According to the Ottoman chronicler Neşri Doğan Beg told Bayezid that 'Our supplies are plentiful, and now that the Sultan is here we shall not be defeated', to which Bayezid supposedly replied 'Hang on bravely, I will look after you. You shall see that I will be here like a flash of lightning!'. The following day the Crusaders slaughtered their prisoners and prepared for battle, only to be totally defeated. After this campaign was over, the garrison commander Doğan Beg was given the title of *Shuja'a al-Din* or 'Hero of the Faith'.

Among the huge number of prisoners taken by the Ottomans after their victory at Nikopol was a young German squire named Johann Schiltberger. He later described his remarkable adventures across much of the Islamic east, one of the first being at Gallipoli:

> Then we were taken by sea to a city called Kalipoli; it is a city where the Turks cross the sea, and there three hundred of us remained for two months confined in a tower. The Duke of Burgundy also was there in the upper part of the tower with those prisoners he had saved; and whilst we were there, King Sigismund passed up on his way to Windischy land [Croatia]. When the Turks heard this, they took us out of the tower and led us to the sea, and one after the other they abused the king and mocked him, and called to him to come out of the boat and deliver his people; and this they did to make fun of him, and skirmished a long time with each other on the sea. But they did not do him any harm, and so he went away.

The Ottomans were probably using cannon by the late 14th century. However the first confirmed use of firearms in defence of an Ottoman fortification was in 1424, when the Karamanid Turkish *emir* Mehmet Bey was killed by a cannon shot while attacking Ottoman-held Antalya. Thereafter, the main Ottoman fortifications were all armed with guns, some of them exceptionally large. The Ottomans' love of huge cannon was particularly useful in defence of naval bases and in their efforts to dominate the Bosphoros and Dardanelles. Until that was achieved, European shipping could pass through with relative ease. The Italian humanist scholar Cyriacus of Ancona described his passage from Constantinople (Istanbul) to Imroz in September 1444, in typically flowery prose:

> ...we plowed the liquid field of peaceful Neptune for three days and nights under winds that blew from the north-east and north, until we arrived at the Hellespont [Dardanelles] and came in sight of the pontifical Christian fleet near ancient Lampsacus. Under the command of Loredan, it was blockading Gallipoli in the Chersonese... That same day, the 27th of September, a bright Sunday, rejoicing in increasingly favouring winds, we passed through the Hellespont, noting that both the European and the Asiatic shores of the Hellespont are guarded strategically by our galleys.

Given Christian naval dominance, the Ottoman fleet based in Gallipoli had to remain under the protection of the port's fortifications. The Ottoman sieges of the Byzantine imperial capital of Constantinople were, in contrast, offensive operations. Yet they also highlighted the importance the Ottomans attached to new fortifications as part of their blockade. Murad II's siege early in the 15th century had shown that Bayezid's castle of Anadolu Hisari was adequate, so Mehmet II determined on something much more ambitious in preparation for his successful siege in 1453. Anadolu Hisari was strengthened, but more importantly the huge new fortress of Rumeli Hisari was erected in nominally Byzantine territory on the opposite shore. If any single event can be said to have marked the doom of Constantinople it was the firing of a 275kg stone cannon ball from a battery of great guns at Rumeli Hisari on 25 November 1452. This sank a three-masted Venetian cargo galley attempting to bring grain from north of the Black Sea to the Byzantine capital.

The next two centuries were characterized by offensive rather than defensive Ottoman siege warfare. Yet Ottoman garrisons sometimes faced serious threats as when, in 1469, the Venetians sacked Enez at the mouth of the river Marica. Five years later they sacked the outer part of Antalya, though they were unable to take the main fortress. Clearly the Janissary garrisons defended such places vigorously. They stood to suffer if they did not,

This anonymous late 17th-century Venetian painting of a sea battle between Venetians and Ottoman galleys off the Aegean coast of Turkey in June 1689 provides a remarkably accurate and detailed illustration of the fortified port of Çesme. (Museo Civico Correr, Venice)

and in 1476, for example, those who escaped after surrendering one fortress were executed by drowning.

The Ottomans' traditionally close cooperation between fleets and forts became yet more sophisticated in the 16th century, though it was not always successful. The Lepanto campaign, which culminated in a massive Ottoman naval defeat in 1571, involved careful logistical preparation by the Ottoman fleet and several major coastal fortresses as well as the gathering of intelligence concerning the enemy's whereabouts and movements. In particular, provisions for six months were assembled for the navy and the fortress of Hersek-Nova at the entrance to the Gulf of Cattaro. The importance of this fortress was further emphasised when Ahmed Paşa, the commander of land forces, was ordered to assemble the *sipahis* of Rumelia (the European provinces) under Beylerbeyi Hüseyin, ready to move rapidly wherever needed, while the *bey* of Küstendil was sent to strengthen the defence of Hersek-Nova. Defeat at Lepanto was nevertheless unexpected, and led the Ottoman Empire to hurriedly complete and garrison various coastal fortresses, including those of southern Anatolia and recently conquered Cyprus.

The chronicler Naima illustrates the bitter nature of siege warfare once the Ottomans reached the limits of their expansion in Europe. For example, on what is now the frontier of Slovakia and Hungary, the castle of Fülek was retaken by the Hapsburgs in 1001 AH (1592/93), to be followed by Szécsény:

> Such of the inhabitants of Fülek as chose to leave it went to Szécsény, but the commander and troops of that fortress were thrown into such a panic on hearing of the infidels that they all fled, carrying with them what they could conveniently take away. The enemy found it of course forsaken and immediately placed a garrison of 500 men in it. The troops in Sunta [Szöny?], in the country of Moravia, also fled for fear of the enemy, and went into the surrounding mountains; but their commander, and about ten men, had the courage to remain where they were. When the enemy appeared before Sunta, the commander and his ten men commenced firing their cannon, in order to lead them to suppose that the fortress was well supplied with men; and in fact this strategem succeeded so far as to awe them; and a report happened to circulate that some thousands of Tatars were on their march to aid the fortress, causing the enemy to retreat

altogether, when the fugitive troops returned to their duty.

Pocitelj, on what is now the frontier between Croatia and Bosnia-Herzegovina, had long been a debateable frontier zone. Its castle fell to the Ottomans in 1496, after which it was strengthened with a polygonal gun tower in the 16th century. (Author's photograph)

The Ottomans may have been on the defensive in Central Europe but they still had huge ambitions north of the Black Sea. One of their most remarkable campaigns was in 1570 when an attempt was made to excavate a canal between the Don and Volga rivers to link the Black and Caspian Seas. This operation was undertaken in open steppe country where fortifications were needed to secure Ottoman supplies, communications and the men digging the canal. About 3,000 Crimean Tatars led by their ruler, Khan Devlet Giray I, joined an army of 10,000 troops and 6,000 labourers under Kasim Paşa. The fortified coastal towns of the Crimea and a few fortresses around Sea of Azov were already under direct Ottoman rule. Beyond these, however the Crimean Khans competed for domination over the steppes with pro-Russian Cossacks and the Khanate of Astrakhan, which had been under Russian control since 1557.

Unfortunately, Khan Devlet Giray was not keen on the idea of permanently garrisoned Ottoman fortresses being established in these areas and so sabotaged the entire project. Nevertheless, the Ottoman expedition excavated about one-third of the canal before winter halted work. The army then marched against Astrakhan but the impossibly cold conditions and fear of an approaching Russian army obliged Kasim Paşa to burn his wooden fortifications and withdraw.

The changing character and increasing costs of 16th-century warfare made fortified storage depots increasingly important. Azov was on a very exposed frontier but others, like Mosul, were further from the nearest border. In such places ammunition and other military supplies were stockpiled in huge quantities. Their fortifications were also often built to a very high standard, the work being carried out when the presence of a large Ottoman army provided both engineering expertise and manpower. When a field army was not present, modernization and repair work was hampered by a persistent shortage of money and, on some frontiers, by huge distances and poor communications. For example, the chronicler Ali noted that a million *akçes* were spent during the winter of 1584/85 to improve the defences of Erzerum, which was at that time in a relatively secure area over 150km from the frontier.

In overall terms, the Ottoman Empire lost its military dominance during the 17th century, though it was still able to extend its territory on some frontiers, even in Europe. Meanwhile, competition with Muslim Iran and the rising power of Orthodox Christian Russia remained acute. Once again the colourful chronicles by Naima include fascinating details of life and warfare. Writing on the capture of Naxçivan in the southern Caucasus in 1012 AH (1603/04) he wrote:

1
2
9
5
4
3
11
10
12
13
6
7
8
A
B
C
D
5 0 10 20m
14
15

The Baş Tabia overlooking Mosul, in northern Iraq, was an Ottoman fortress built on the site of a sequence of earlier fortifications. (Author's photograph)

The fortress or city of Naxçivan was a place of no great strength, having been built of weak materials. Most of its buildings were made of clay and mortar; its walls low; and ever since the time the greater part of them were thrown down, provisions had not been very plentiful in it. But it was near to Yerevan,

D RUMELI HISARI

Unlike Anadolu Hisari, Rumeli Hisari was designed to operate with the enlarged earlier fortress to close the Bosphoros with their massive new bronze cannon. These were sited close to the shore, almost at water level, so that their stone cannon balls skipped across the water like pebbles across a pond. Rumeli Hisari's first major action came on 10 November 1452, when its guns opened fire on a pair of Venetian ships, which escaped. The Ottoman gunners adjusted their range and on 25 November they sank a large three-masted Venetian merchant galley that tried to run the blockade.

Key for main picture:

1 Saruca Paşa Tower.
2 Dağ (Mountain) Gate.
3 Dizdaz (Sentries) Gate leading to barbican.
4 Halil Paşa Tower.
5 At the time of the sinking of the Venetian blockade-runner, the fortifications of the barbican were apparently not yet complete and the heavy guns were simply lined up along the shore.
6 The huge stone cannon ball that sank the Venetian blockade-runner was probably not the first shot, the guns' fixed positions suggesting that they were fired in sequence.
7 The doomed Venetian ship was a three-masted merchant galley, not a speedy war galley.
8 The vessel would have tried to sail down the middle of the strait, to keep as far as possible from the guns of both Ottoman fortresses.
9 Su (Water) Tower.
10 Sel (Ravine) Gate was a minor entrance to the fortress.
11 The first mosque in Rumeli Hisari appears to have been a simple wooden building, erected over a large cistern.
12 There are thought to have been at least three wells inside the fortress.
13 The other buildings inside Rumeli Hisari were also simple and functional.

Key for the plan of Rumeli Hisari:

1 The Zağanos Paşa Tower.
2 Water Tower (Su Kulesi).
3 Saruca Paşa Tower.
4 Halil Paşa Tower.
5 Little Zağanos Paşa Tower (Küçük Zağanos Paşa Kulesi).
6 Ravine Gate (Sel Kapisi).
7 Mountain Gate (Dağ Kapisi).
8 Sentries Gate (Dizdaz Kapisi).
9 Barbican Gate (Hisarpeçe Kapisi).
10 Mosque.
11 Cistern.
12 Fountain.
13 Wells.
14 Barbican (built some time later).
15 Ground-level embrasures for heavy cannon.

Key for Saruca Paşa Tower and neighbouring Mountain Gate:

1 Section (A–B) through the tower, with the adjacent Mountain Gate.
2 Section (C–D) through the Mountain Gate.
3 Plan of tower's ground-floor chamber.
4 Plan of tower's upper chamber.
5 Plan of tower's upper gallery and upper central tower.

> and if it happened at any time to be deprived of the aid of the military, and was in danger from enemies, Yerevan formed a near and accessible asylum for their families and property, and whence they might easily annoy their enemies. Yerevan was exceedingly strong and well fortified, having abundance of cannon and provisions within it.

Just because a fortress was on the European frontier did not necessarily mean that it was maintained in an up-to-date manner. The town of Pécs in southern Hungary served as a major regional base, but its defences were largely medieval. Thus a relatively lightly equipped Hapsburg raiding force was able to breach its outer wall early in 1664. According to the chronicler Silahdar Findikli Mehmed Ağa, the breaches remained 'wide enough to allow grazing animals to pass in and out of the city walls without obstruction'.

Small-scale raiding continued to characterize warfare on this front. In fact, ransom from prisoners was now a major source of income for troops on both sides. Amongst the Ottomans some captives were sold for resale in slave markets while others were forced to work locally, often as pioneers in siege warfare. Captured soldiers may have been in a better position than captured peasants, since they were more likely to be ransomed. Such payments were made in kind, in weapons and in money. Christian slave raiding was also a major reason for naval attacks on Ottoman-ruled North Africa, the captives being used as galley slaves. One particularly damaging raid was by the fleet of Ferdinando I di Medici of Florence against the Algerian town of al-Anabas (Bône) in 1607. The Knights of the Order of St Stephen and Tuscan troops who manned this fleet suffered only 47 casualties but captured 1,464 prisoners and claimed to have slaughtered 470 Muslims.

Cooperation between galley squadrons and coastal fortifications remained central to naval strategy during the 17th century. This meant that the Dardanelles, close to the Ottoman capital of Istanbul, became a front line when the Venetians briefly controlled the offshore islands of Lemnos and Bozca-ada (Tenedos) in 1656. Two years later, a Christian fleet assembled at Bozca-ada and advanced against the Dardanelles in the hope of breaking through. Meanwhile, the Ottomans assembled their fleet within the strait, ready to attack Bozca-ada. The Christian fleet then had to sail back to Bozca-ada for drinking water before returning to the Dardanelles. At the same time, the Ottoman fleet advanced. Heavy cannon on the shores forced the Christian fleet to stay in the middle of the strait where they faced the Ottoman fleet. During the savage battle that followed both fleets drifted towards the island of Bozca-ada. Here the Venetians sought shelter

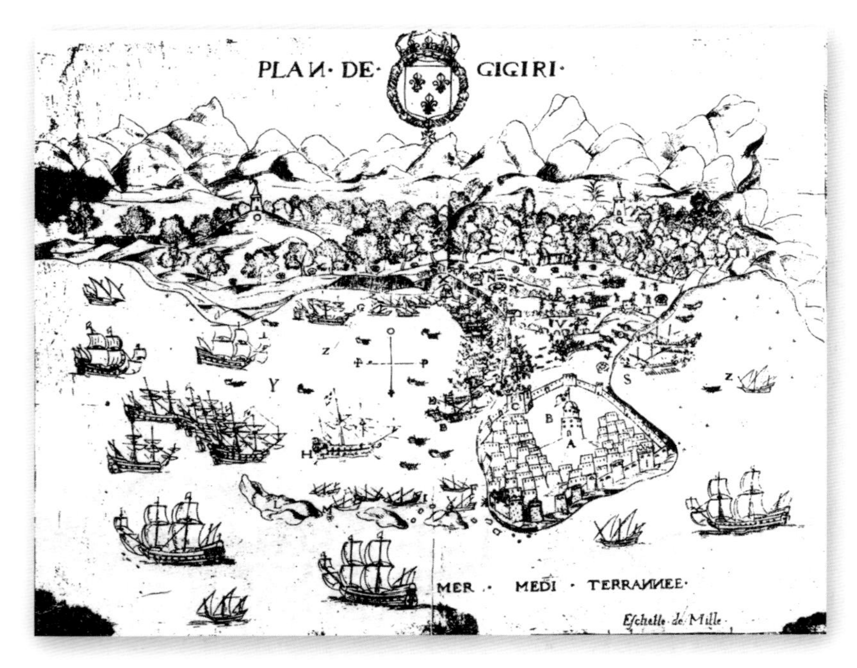

An engraved illustration of the French seizure of Jijel (Gigiri) in Ottoman-ruled Algeria in July 1664 showing the plan of attack as well as the fortified city and harbour. (Algerian National Library, Algiers)

while the Ottoman fleet sailed on towards Lesbos. This left the Christian fleet between the Dardanelles fortresses and the now-battered Ottoman fleet.

During a further clash the following day the Venetian flagship was hit and blew up. Other actions followed but Christian morale now slumped, their surviving commanders quarrelled and various squadrons went home, leaving the Venetians almost alone. They decided to attack Ottoman transport ships in the Dardanelles because these were almost undefended by Ottoman galleys, most of which were moored at Lesbos. Thereupon the Ottoman galleys returned and landed troops on Bozca-ada by night. The Venetians fought on for several days, but finding themselves outmanoeuvred they eventually abandoned the island and retreated. During this time the Ottoman fortifications on the Dardanelles had only fired a few shots, but had fulfilled their purpose admirably. It may, in fact, have been their strategic success that convinced Sultan Mehmet IV to strengthen the Dardanelles still further by having additional fortresses built at Seddülbahir and Kumkale.

Hapsburg pressure upon the Ottomans' Balkan provinces continued throughout most of the 18th century while Russian pressure increased in the Black Sea region. For the Ottoman Empire the importance of fortresses increased accordingly but during sieges their magazines blew up with horrifying frequency. One of the most devastating explosions was at Belgrade, an event commemorated in an inscription on the mortar that actually did the damage, now preserved in the Heeresgeschichtliches Museum in Vienna. The text reads:

> On 14 August 1717 I was planted before the fortress of Belgrade, causing great consternation. And my little bomb must have sped many folk to their deaths. It landed on the powder magazine, and left nothing in the place save lamentation, death, horror and the most frightful ruin.

In fact, the explosion removed the tops of all the minarets in Belgrade and is said to have killed 3,000 people.

The morale of Ottoman garrisons nevertheless remained high, despite losses of territory. This was noted by the Hapsburg commander, Count Kinsky. In his book published in 1790 he wrote that '...when the Turk is fighting for his fortress he is also fighting for his fortune, for his goods and chattels, for his wife and children, and for his mosque. Although they have no idea of the art of defence, they put up a fierce resistance in their castles and fortresses, reposing their trust in their personal strength and bravery and in the number of their men.'

Even though the Turkish naval hero Gazi Hassan of Algiers won a local success against the Russian fleet in the northern Aegean in 1770, the Ottomans realised that a failure in this area could prove fatal. So the sultan recruited the best foreign advisors he could find, including the Franco-Hungarian Baron De Tott. His first action was to withdraw the Ottoman fleet deeper into the Dardanelles and to line both shores, between the 'old' and 'new' pairs of fortresses with further artillery and mortar batteries. However, the Ottomans still loved their massive ancient cannon and resisted some of De Tott's modernization efforts.

The psychological impact of these mighty weapons was undeniable, as noted by the French traveller D'Irumberry, who passed through the Dardanelles by night in April 1791 and could not avoid thinking of the 'terrible pieces of artillery' with which the 'two forts bristled'. They were also more effective then might have been expected, as the British found in 1807. This campaign started badly for the Royal Navy when one of Admiral

Securing a garrison's supply of drinking water was solved in a different manner at the Baba Vida castle in Vidin. Knowing that an enemy may win control of the neighbouring river Danube, the Ottomans built this polygonal tower over a well a short distance from the riverbank. (Author's photograph)

E

The Fortress of Seddülbahir in the late 18th century

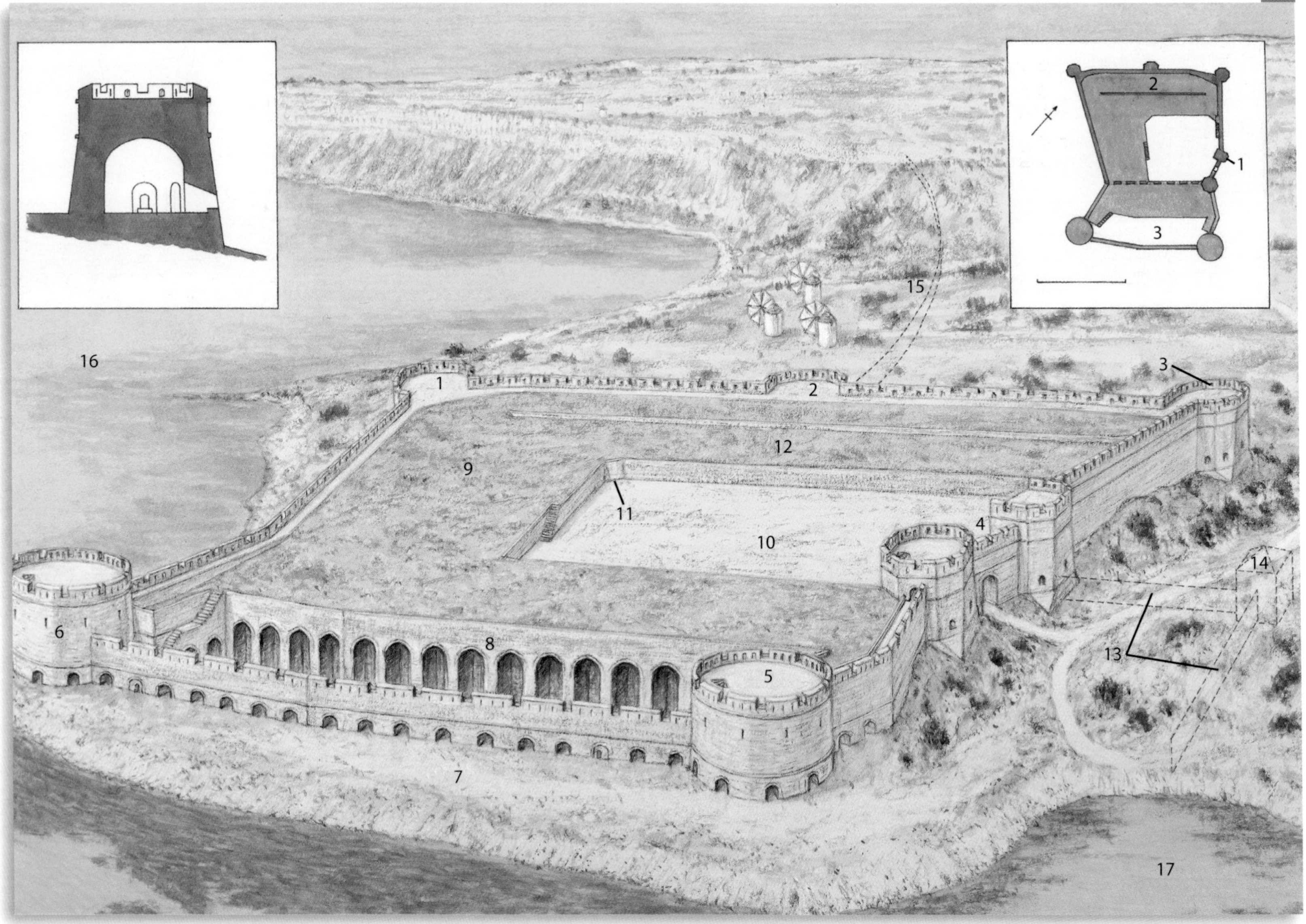

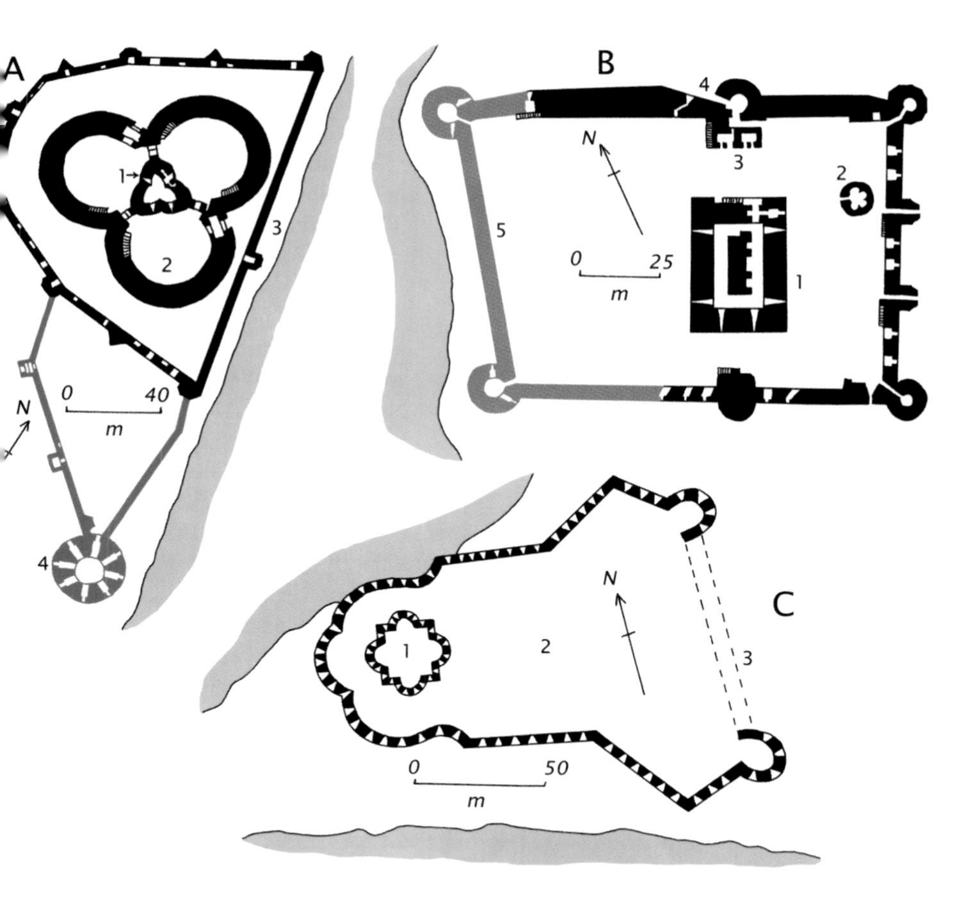

A: Kilidülbahir, 15th century fortress in black, 16th century additions in red (after Curcic): **(1)** trefoil-shaped keep started by Mehmet II in 1452; **(2)** trilobate inner castle started by Mehmet II in 1452; **(3)** outer walls of the original fortress with shore batteries, probably started by Mehmet II in 1452; **(4)** artillery tower and southern extension built for Sultan Sulëyman I, mid-16th century.
B: Kale-i Sultaniye, Canakkale, 15th-century fortress in black, partially demolished and buried western defences in grey (after Turkish Antiquaries Authorities): **(1)** central keep; **(2)** powder magazine; **(3)** Mosque of Sultan Mehmet II; **(4)** main entrance; **(5)** the now-hidden western towers and neighbouring walls had numerous embrasures.
C: Nağara Kalesi (based upon historical and satellite photographs): **(1)** central artillery tower, built for Sultan Selim III around 1807; **(2)** outer enclosure, built for Selim III or Mahmut II; **(3)** whether the eastern wall of the fort was ever completed remains unclear.

E THE FORTRESS OF SEDDÜLBAHIR IN THE LATE 18TH CENTURY

From the 15th century onwards, the defences of the Dardanelles strait were designed in pairs, with one fortification on the European and one on the Asian side. Until the 20th century, cannon in the outermost fortresses of Seddülbahir and Kumkale could not cover the distance between them. Nevertheless, both were primarily intended as artillery positions. Today Seddülbahir consists of three elements, dating from the mid-17th, 18th and late 19th centuries. The first enclosure, with its octagonal towers, was built in 1659 under Sultan Mehmet IV. Its towers and walls had characteristic horizontal lines of bulging masonry, the uppermost running beneath the crenellations, while the octagonal towers rested on rectangular bases. There were also gun ports low down the sides of these towers. The 18th-century addition perhaps resulted in the disappearance of a southern tower. This extension consisted of an extended bastion with a relatively low wall with gun ports along the shore. The two round towers at the ends of this sea wall are similarly pierced by ground-level gun ports.

Key to main picture:

1 Polygonal western tower.
2 Polygonal northwestern tower.
3 Polygonal northern tower.
4 Gate complex.
5 Round eastern tower.
6 Round southern tower.
7 Sea wall pierced for sea-level artillery.
8 Open space for heavy artillery.
9 Earth-fill covering most of the interior of the fortress.
10 Lower level area within retaining wall, accessed through main gate.
11 Entrances in corners, leading to storage areas and perhaps to the corner towers.
12 Additional retaining wall to support earth-fill behind the northwestern wall.
13 Possible position of an additional external wall shown on an 18th-century European engraving,
14 Possible position of a simple tower also shown on an 18th-century European engraving.
15 Possible position of an additional external wall shown on an 18th-century European engraving, apparently extending to the Ilyasbaba Burnu headland.
16 Aegean Sea.
17 Entrance to the Dardanelles Strait.

Key to hypothetical plan of Seddülbahir in the late 18th century:

1 Entrance.
2 Retaining wall to support earth-fill behind northwestern wall.
3 Open space for heavy artillery.

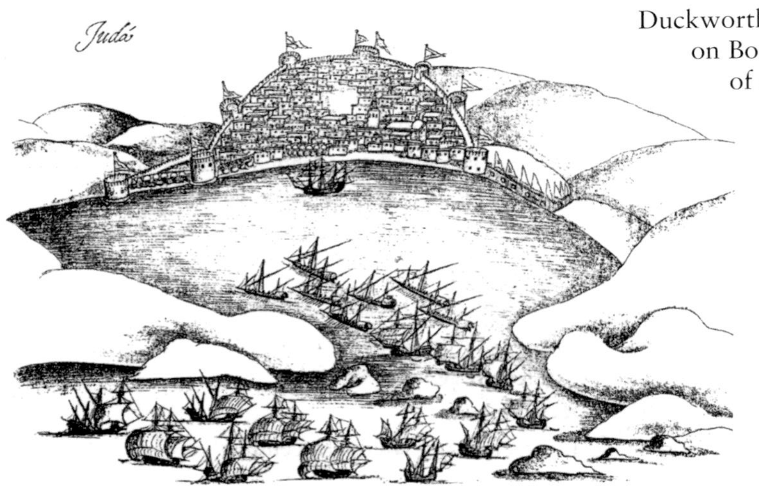

The original appearance of the Ottoman Red Sea port of Jeddah is shown in this 16th-century Portuguese engraving. (Biblioteca Central de Marinha, Lisbon)

Duckworth's ships caught fire, drifted ashore on Bozca-ada and blew up with the deaths of about 250 men. On 18 February the wind turned and the British entered the Dardanelles with nine ships-of-the-line and two bomb vessels. This sudden attack – without a declaration of war – caught the outer forts by surprise. It was also the holy month of Ramadan, so only skeleton garrisons were on duty. Nevertheless, they opened fire and were answered by the bomb vessels. As the British sailed deeper into the strait the inner forts also opened fire but were answered by every British ship. Just beyond the inner forts a small Ottoman squadron was moored against the Asian shore. Only one small vessel escaped while the others fired upon the British. Most of Duckworth's fleet anchored about 5km further into the Dardanelles, while five British warships destroyed the Ottoman squadron and landed troops to demolish an artillery battery in the as-yet incomplete fort on Nağara point. By this point the British had lost ten men killed and 77 wounded.

Several weeks cruising outside Istanbul proved fruitless. Meanwhile, Sultan Selim III hurried troops, engineers and advisors from the French embassy under Napoleon's agent Horace Sebastiani to the Dardanelles. Here they strengthened the fortifications, installed guns and brought the garrisons up to something like full strength. At the start of March, Admiral Duckworth eventually realised that he was in danger of being trapped so, having assembled his ships, he ran the gauntlet of the Dardanelles again. This time the British had the current and wind with them, but the Ottoman defenders were also ready and waiting. Their actions were directed by Vice Consul Mechain from the French embassy who now observed the British retreat from the hill behind Nağara point, sending runners to warn the various forts of the British fleet's movements. Almost every British ship was hit, some by stone cannon balls weighing over 350kg. Though none were disabled or sunk, another 29 crew members were killed, 138 were injured and four went missing.

AFTERMATH

Sultan Selim III's attempts to reform the Ottoman Empire's military strength appeared to have failed when he was overthrown in 1807. Yet his successor, Mustafa IV, reigned only briefly and was soon succeeded by another, more successful reformer: Mahmud II. He reigned until 1839, during which period the Ottoman state began a transformation that enabled it to survive until 1922. Yet even as late as 1828 the Italian Major-General Valentini could write that: 'They have no idea of a regular system either of bastions or of lines, or outworks or covered ways, nor of conforming the height of the works to the nature of the ground in front. When we find anything of this kind in a Turkish fortress, we may be assured that it has been in the hands of some European power, by which it has been improved or originally constructed.'

Within the Ottoman Empire's Balkan provinces traditional and modern fortifications continued to exist side by side, and during the first Serbian uprising of 1804–13 the rebels made widespread use of earth-and-timber forts, which were simply updated *palankas*. Now called *haidouk* forts, these usually incorporated wooden corner towers and taller central structures surrounded by a wooden curtain wall. Some pre-Ottoman and Ottoman fortifications were ruthlessly modernized. One of the greatest losses was the demolition in 1896 of the medieval fortified bridge, tower and drawbridge linking the Greek island of Evvoia to the mainland. Elsewhere, geographical and man-made changes helped preserve medieval and early Ottoman fortifications such as those of Enez at the mouth of the river Marica. Silting of the estuary eventually destroyed its importance as a port. It was bypassed by a railway, while new frontiers reduced Enez to a small fishing village on a tense Turkish–Greek frontier. In fact it is only recently that Enez has emerged from its centuries-old military past.

The interior of one of the main bastions of the Kara Baba fortress, which was built in 1686 to dominate the narrow channel between the Greek mainland and the island of Evvoia. (Author's photograph)

Throughout the 19th and 20th centuries the strategic importance of the Dardanelles and Bosphoros Straits ensured that their outer fortifications were modernized whereas some of the older fortifications deeper within the straits lost their military significance. Rumeli Hisari, for example, became a civilian village, its 15th-century Ebulfeth Mosque being destroyed by fire in 1907. The villagers were relocated 46 years later, and in 1958 Rumeli Hisari was opened to tourists.

No attention was paid to the admittedly less impressive Bigali Kalesi. Despite being strengthened by Sultan Mahmut II, it was never very important and was soon left to crumble away in peace. In contrast, the Kale-i Sultaniyye at Canakkale remained key to the defence of the Dardanelles until World War I. Its seaward side was rebuilt in the late 19th century as a row of artillery positions instead of a fortified wall, which had the unfortunate effect of attracting the attention of the British and French fleets in 1915. The damage they caused was relatively minor but a huge, unexploded shell fired by HMS *Queen Elizabeth* remains embedded within the Kale-i Sultaniyye's northern wall.

Within Anatolia the only earlier Ottoman fortifications to have been seriously modernized were those along the Caucasus frontier with Russia. Here Kars fell to the Russians, who substantially strengthened its citadel. The same was true of various fortresses within what are now Armenia, Georgia, Azerbaijan and the Caucasus republics of the Russian Federation. North of the Black Sea the great Ottoman fortress of Yeni-Kale was formally ceded to Russia by the Treaty Küçük Kaynarca in 1774. However,

LEFT
During the later Middle Ages, Enez on the coast of Turkish Thrace was a strongly fortified outpost of the Genoese colonial empire. It surrendered to the Ottomans three years after the fall of Constantinople, after which the massive citadel of Enez was garrisoned by Ottoman troops. (Author's photograph)

RIGHT
Bigali Kalesi is perhaps the last example of a classic rectangular Ottoman fort with vertical stone walls and medieval-style embrasures. It was built for Sultan Selim III in or shortly after 1807 to further strengthen the defence of the Dardanelles. (Author's photograph)

the newcomers used it as a military hospital and added virtually nothing to the fortifications. Far to the south in Iraq the once impressive Azamiye Kalesi in Baghdad, built by Sultan Süleyman the Magnificent in 1534, lost its importance during the 19th century and gradually disappeared as streets were widened and neighbouring buildings were extended, so that virtually nothing now remains.

The situation in Syria, Lebanon and Jordan was different. Here most Ottoman military architecture was virtually ignored, with the exception of the Hajj forts, particularly those in Jordan, and some quasi-fortified *hans* along the old Ottoman trade routes. In Palestine the late 18th-century palace and citadel of Acre were converted into a prison during the 19th century, but have since been restored by the Israelis. The fortifications of the Old City of Jerusalem may always have been more symbolic than real, and their preservation in good repair was usually

F THE BAB AL-QULLA COMPLEX IN THE CITADEL OF CAIRO

Much of today's Citadel of Cairo dates from the centuries of Ottoman rule, or from the 19th century when Egypt was a virtually independent state under nominal Ottoman authority. The most important change made by the Ottomans was to the 16th-century fortifications that separated the Northern and Southern Enclosures. They separated the Janissary garrison in the Northern Enclosure from rival Ottoman units. On the left of this picture the Burj al-Tabbalin (Drummers' Tower), now called the Bab al-Wustani (Middle Tower), overlooked one entrance to the Citadel and part of the city where the once-dominant Mamluks lived. On the right the Burj al-Suffa (now called the Burj al-Muqattam) is the highest tower in the Citadel. Its cannon overlooked the *Haush* (governor's palace). The space between the 14th-century mosque of Sultan al-Nasir mosque (on the far right) and the gate leading to the Northern Enclosure had been used as a parade ground during the Mamluk era. Much of it was later covered by shops and markets.

1. Bab al-Mudarraj (Gate of the Steps), replaced by the Bab al-Jadid (New Gate) in 1828.
2. Burj al-Ahmar (Red Tower).
3. Artillery platform.
4. Mosque of Sülayman Paşa (1528).
5. Burj al-Haddad (Blackmith's Tower).
6. Burj al-Ramla (Sand Tower).
7. Burj al-Imam (Rector's Tower).
8. Burj al-Turfa (Masterpiece Tower).
9. Burj al-Muqattam (Tower of Muqattam), named after the neighbouring Muqattam Hill (16th century).
10. Bir Yusuf (Joseph's Well), defended by two new Ottoman towers (probably 16th century).
11. Mosque of al-Nasir.
12. Bab al-Qulla, 16th century.
13. Burj al-Wustani (Middle Tower), 16th century.
14. Bab al-Wustani (Middle Gate), added in 1826.
15. Tomb of Shaykh Muhammad al-Ka'ki (16th century).
16. Bab al-Jabal (Mountain Gate), added in 1786.
17. Burj al-Inkishariyya (Janissaries Tower), demolished in the 19th century.

F The Bab al-Qulla complex in the Citadel of Cairo

- BROWN: Ottoman fortifications, buildings and major alterations.
- BLUE: During the late 17th and 18th centuries, the interior of the Northern Enclosure was largely filled with domestic, craft or business buildings, turning it into a residential area.
- GREY: Original fortifications and other buildings dating from the Ayyubid and Mamluk periods (late 12th to early 16th centuries)

The Yeni-Kale on the Kerch peninsular, at the easternmost tip of the Crimea, was a new fortress built by the Ottomans between 1699 and 1706. An Italian convert to Islam, named Goloppo, is largely credited with its design. (Clipper photograph)

seen by the authorities as a religiously correct and politically important act.

In Jordan a new form of fortification appeared in the late 18th century, comparable to the *konaği* fortified great houses of Anatolia. Many served as 'tribal strongholds' and were like grand versions of other village structures. One is al-Alali, of the Shraydih family who dominated Tibnih. It is a two-storey groin-vaulted construction entered through an impressive pointed arch. Though it incorporates an upstairs prayer room, al-Alali lacks the inner courtyard that is almost universal in other parts of 'Greater Syria'.

Most changes to Ottoman fortifications in 19th-century Egypt resulted from political rather than military modernization. For example, in 1826 the entrance through the Bab al-Qulla gateway in the Citadel of Cairo was widened to enable Egypt's de facto independent ruler, Muhammad Ali, to drive through in his new European-style carriage. Several Ottoman fortifications in Arabia were, however, strengthened as a result of continuing attempts to consolidate Ottoman control over this turbulent region. One was the Ecyad ('Ajyad' in Arabic) Kalesi, built in Mecca around 1781. Enclosing an area of 23,000m^2 on Bulbul Mountain, it defended the Kaaba and neighbouring Islamic shrines. This huge fort was nevertheless demolished by the Saudi Arabian government in 2002, causing considerable anger in Turkey. The greatest damage to Ottoman fortifications in North Africa was done during the French invasion and under French rule, most notably in Algeria. Those that remained

Security within the Ottoman Empire meant that traditional merchant *hans* did not need to be as defensible as they used to be. This German or Italian drawing illustrates a typical example and dates from the 16th century. (National Bibliotek, Vienna)

then underwent extensive modernization and only a small number of the once-abundant Ottoman forts now survive.

THE SITES TODAY

The regions still possessing Ottoman fortifications are mostly now accessible to visitors, though some of the borders between them remain closed. For example it is currently impossible to cross the land frontier between Turkey and Armenia, while it is, of course, similarly impossible to travel directly between Syria and Israel. Iraq is only tentatively returning as a destination for dedicated 'cultural tourists'; similarly all the Balkan and Central European countries are now 'open', including Albania. This previously closed land with its rich historical and architectural heritage, superb scenery and virtually untouched coastline, will surely become a major Mediterranean destination.

Many of the most impressive examples of Ottoman military architecture are in Turkey where the fortifications of the Bosphoros and Dardanelles are a 'must see', not least because their dates span most of the period in question. Some have been made presentable as tourist destinations and only a few remain inaccessible. For example, Anadolu Hisari can only be inspected from outside, and despite having been restored in 1991–93, the interior currently remains closed to the public. The much later fort at Nağara Kalesi cannot even be approached closely as it remains a Turkish Army position, monitoring traffic through the Dardanelles. The fortifications can, of course, be seen from a ship, but the use of a conspicuous telephoto lens is not recommended. The citadel of Kars, having served as a Cold War base for the Turkish Army on the frontier with the Soviet Union, remains somewhat sensitive, though it can be visited. Elsewhere in Turkey, the overwhelming majority of Ottoman fortifications are accessible, though sometimes difficult to reach.

Until recently, most Balkan countries had an ambivalent attitude towards the Ottoman period. In Bulgaria, Serbia and Greece this resulted in various 'Turkish' architectural monuments, whether military, civilian or religious, being demolished as late as the 1950s. In general, however, fortifications from the Ottoman period were either ignored, misidentified or were still used as military positions. Bulgaria, once the very heart of the Ottoman Empire's European territories, preserves several interesting examples of Ottoman military architecture, including a gate in the southeast part of the city wall of Rusçuk. The Baba Vida castle in Vidin is largely late-medieval Bulgarian, but its outer fortifications are mostly Ottoman, as are three of its gates: the Istanbul gate, the Pazar Gate and the Boqlug Gate.

As the Aegean and Mediterranean coasts of Turkey are increasingly developed for tourism, their coastal forts tend to be incorporated into new tourist facilities. This process was already under way in the 1980s, when a camping and caravanning site was set up next to the octagonal Ottoman fort at Ağa Liman near Silifke. (Author's photograph)

By 1963, when this photograph was taken, the buildings within the Yediküle fortress had been demolished, leaving only a minaret and a water cistern. (Author's photograph)

With few exceptions, Ottoman fortifications in Greece are open to the public, though they rarely rate as major tourist destinations, and a few are still within military zones or are used as prisons. Elsewhere in the Balkans the most common problem with such Ottoman military monuments is their inaccessibility. Then there is the fact that the majority of specifically Ottoman fortifications, particularly those in the frontier regions of the northern Balkans and Central Europe, were of the *palanka* type. All that remain of these are barely discernible earthworks and, as far as the author is aware, no attempt has been made to reconstruct a *palanka* in the way that several earth-and-timber fortifications have been rebuilt in Russia.

BELOW
The beautiful bridge that spanned the river in Mostar was destroyed by Christian gunners during the Bosnian civil war. Less attention was paid to the 16th- and 17th-century fortified Ottoman tower that dominated one end of the bridge. (Author's photograph)

Stone and brick fortifications from the Ottoman period exist in Romania, and include some fortified monasteries in Moldavia. However, these are justifiably presented as 'Romanian' rather than Ottoman since they were almost all constructed under the patronage of autonomous local rulers. A number of fine, but as yet little-known, examples of military architecture from this period exist in Moldova, Ukraine and to a lesser extent the Black Sea coastal regions of Russia. Here, however, the Ottomans usually added to or modernized these positions, and thus their contribution tends to be downgraded by 'patriotic' local tourist boards. Only when the Ottomans built something significant from scratch, as they did at Yeni-Kale in the Crimea, are the 'Turks' given proper credit.

Hungary was a strongly fortified kingdom during the late medieval period. It is therefore quite difficult to find specifically Ottoman fortifications because, with the exception of numerous but now virtually invisible *palankas*, the Ottomans again merely strengthened what they found in place. On the other hand, the Hungarians have a more positive attitude towards the 'Ottoman occupation' than most other peoples in Europe, so Ottoman constructions are properly and fully identified. Several are found in Hungary's wine-growing territory, and in fact the name of one famous Hungarian wine recalls a siege during Süleyman the Magnificent's invasion of Hungary. According to this legend, the Hungarian garrison defending Eger was given abundant local red wine to maintain its morale. The Turks were then supposedly told that the heroic resistance of this garrison came from the fact that bulls' blood was mixed with their wine. Many of the fortifications that so often changed hands between the Ottomans and their Hapsburg foes now lie within southern Slovakia. In most cases, however, what remains largely dates from before or after Ottoman rule.

Ottoman fortifications are more difficult to identify in the Caucasus and western Iran, largely because they mostly consisted of improvements to existing defences and tended to be built in a style traditional to those regions. Many within what are now the Caucasus republics and southern Russia were also substantially altered after the Russian conquest.

The situation is different within the Arab world, and although little is known to survive in Iraq, future investigation might identify other structures as Ottoman. At present the most obvious fortification from these centuries is the much-damaged Citadel of Mosul. A recent warming of relations between Syria and Turkey has had an unexpected impact upon several Ottoman monuments in Syria, including the famous *tekke* in Damascus where Hajj caravans and their guards assembled before a hazardous journey to Medina and Mecca. As a result, the 'unsuitable' Syrian Military Museum was moved elsewhere following comments by the visiting Turkish President.

In Lebanon, most existing Ottoman military architecture again consists of modifications to earlier structures. The main exception is a number of partially fortified 'great houses' built by powerful families in what was, throughout the Ottoman period, the virtually independent province of Mount Lebanon. Most of these buildings are still in the hands of powerful families and as such remain centres of political, and in some respects also military, power.

The medieval citadel of Kars was greatly strengthened by the Ottomans in the 16th century and then again by the Russians who occupied Kars from 1878 until 1918. (Author's photograph)

In addition to the two great towers, intervening wall and new Bab al-Qulla gate separating the northern and southern enclosures of the Citadel of Cairo, the Ottomans also strengthened the defences around the 12th-century Bir Yusuf or 'Joseph's Well', adding this polygonal artillery tower. (Author's photograph)

The most distinctive Ottoman military buildings in Jordan are forts along the Hajj road to the Hijaz region of western Arabia. Until modern times they were difficult to reach, but then the famous Hijaz Railway was built close to the Ottoman Hajj route. More recently the Jordanian government built the Desert Highway along a similar line, at least as far as Ma'an where it separates to head for the port of Aqaba rather than the Islamic Holy Cities. Today this is a major road, and many of the Ottoman Hajj forts are just a short walk away. One also benefitted from the long-established and close relationship between Jordan and Turkey, the ruins of Zahr Unayza having been stabilized and made presentable for visitors at Turkish expense.

The Ottoman Hajj forts in Saudi Arabia are more difficult to reach, but the task is not impossible. There are also examples of Arabian 'tribal fortification' from the period of somewhat nominal Ottoman rule elsewhere in the kingdom, though their design and construction rarely owes much to Ottoman influence. The same goes for those few forts along the Persian Gulf coast that occasionally housed Ottoman garrisons. The Ottoman presence in Yemen was more deep-seated, though again intermittent. Here, virtually no scholarly work has been done on fortifications that could be categorized as Ottoman. Although most of Yemen's existing fortifications date from early modern rather than medieval or ancient times, their design is almost entirely traditional and again owes little to the Ottoman presence.

Most surviving Ottoman fortifications in Egypt are concentrated in Cairo and near Alexandria. As such they are easy to reach and are open to the public, especially as the Nile Delta region no longer has so many of the military checkpoints which made travel so difficult during the second half of the 20th century. Ottoman forts or remains of forts on the Red Sea coast and in Sinai require greater effort but are again mostly accessible. In neighbouring Libya the situation for visitors is improving at a remarkable rate. Ottoman military and other architecture is concentrated along the Mediterranean coast and is mostly found in the cities, particularly Tripoli. The same is true of Tunisia and Algeria, the former being better supplied with modern hotels and travel facilities than the latter, though it is less interesting where forts and fortifications associated with the so-called 'Barbary Pirates' are concerned.

BIBLIOGRAPHY

Agoston, G., 'The Costs of the Ottoman Fortress System in Hungary in the Sixteenth and Seventeeth Centuries' in *Ottomans, Hungarians and Habsburgs in Central Europe: The Military Confines in the Era of Ottoman Conquest*, Brill, Leiden, (2000) pp.195–228

Aksan, V. H., 'Manning a Black Sea Garrison in the 18th Century', in J. Hathaway (ed.), *Mutiny and Rebellion in the Ottoman Empire*, University of Wisconsin-Madison, Madison, (2002) pp.63–72

Alexander, J., 'Qalat Sai: the most southerly Ottoman fortress in Africa' in *Sudan and Nubia*, 1 (1997) pp.16–20

Barbir, K. K., *Ottoman Rule in Damascus 1708–1758*, Princeton University Press, Princeton (1980)

Curcic, S. and Hadjitryphonos, E. (eds.), *Secular Medieval Architecture in the Balkans 1300–1500, and its preservation*, AIMOS, Thessaloniki (1997)

De Tott (ed. F. Tóth), *Mémoires du Baron de Tott sur les Turcs et les Tartares, Maestricht, 1785*, H. Champion, Paris (2004)

Djelloul, N., *Les fortifications cotières ottomans de la Régence de Tunis*, Fondation Temimi pour la Recherche Scientifique et l'Information, Zaghouan (1995)

Foss, C., *Ephesus after Antiquity: A late antique, Byzantine and Turkish City*, Cambridge University Press, Cambridge (1979)

Gabriel, A., *Châteaux turcs du Bosphore*, Editions de Boccard, Paris (1943)

Gradeva, R., 'War and Peace along the Danube: Vidin at the End of the Seventeenth Century' in *Oriente Moderno*, 81 (2001) pp.149–75

Harrison, P., 'Castles and Fortresses of the Peleponnese, from Justinian until Greek Independence' in *Fortress*, 17 (1993) pp.3–20

Hawari, M., 'The Citadel (Qal'a) in the Ottoman Period: An Overview' in *Ottoman Jerusalem: The Living City, 1517–1917, vol. I*, Altajar, London (2000) pp.493–518

Hawari, M., Auld, H. and Hudson, J., 'Qal'at Burak. A Fort of the Ottoman Period south of Bethlehem' in *Levant*, 32 (2000) pp.101–20

Hegyi, K., 'The Ottoman Network of Fortresses in Hungary' in *Ottomans, Hungarians and Habsburgs in Central Europe: The Military Confines in the Era of Ottoman Conquest*, Brill, Leiden, (2000) pp.163–93

Hertz, A. Z., 'Ada Kale: Key to the Danube' in *Archivum Ottomanicum*, 3 (1971) pp.170–184

——, 'Armament and Supply inventory of Ottoman Ada Kale, 1753' in *Archivum Ottomanicum*, 4 (1972) pp.95–171

Hillenbrand, R., *The Architecture of Ottoman Jerusalem: An Introduction*, Al Tajir World of Islam Trust, London (2002)

Högg, H., *Türkenburgen an Bosporus und Hellespont*, Focken & Oltmanns, Dresden (1932)

Kiel, M., 'A Note on the Exact date of Construction of the White Tower of Thessaloniki' in *Balkan Studies*, 14 (1973) pp.352–57

——, 'The Building Accounts of the Castle of Vlorë/Avlonya (S. Albania) 1537–1539' in *Proceedings of the second International Congress on the Ottoman Culture in the Balkans, Tirana, December 2003*, Research Center for IslamicHistory, Art and Culture, Istanbul (2006) pp.3–31.

——, 'The Construction of the Ottoman Castle of Anavarin-i Cedid according to the orders of the Imperial Council... (June 1572 – November 1577)' in *A Historical and Economic Geography of Ottoman Greece, Hesperia Supplement*, 34, American School of Classical Studies in Athens, Athens (2005) pp.265–81

Lawless, R. I., 'Berat and Gjirocaster: Two Museum Towns of Albania' in *Islam in the Balkans*, The Royal Scottish Museum, Edinburgh (1979) pp.9–17

Moulay Belhamissi, *Marine et Marins d'Alger (151–1830)*, 3 vols, Bibliothèque Nationale d'Algerie, Algiers (1996)

Murphey, R., 'The Construction of a Fortress at Mosul in 1631: A Case Study of an Important Facet of Ottoman Military Expenditure', in *Social and Economic History of Turkey (1071–1920)*, Meteksan, Ankara (1980) pp.163–77

Petersen, A., 'Ottoman Hajj Forts' in *The Archaeology of Jordan*, Sheffield University Press, Sheffield (2001) pp.686–91

Quesne, C. Le, *Quseir: An Ottoman and Napoleonic Fortress on the Red Sea Coast of Egypt*, The American University in Cairo, Cairo (2007)

Riza, E., 'L'habitation fortifiee de Gjirokaster' in *Monumentet*, 1, Tirana (1971) pp.145–47

Römer, C., *Osmanische Festungsbesatzungen in Ungarn zur Zeit Murads III* (Garrison life on the Ottoman frontier in Hungary), Österreichischen Akademie der Wissenschaften, Vienna (1995)

Savvides, A. G. C., 'Constantinople in a vice: Some notes on Anadolu Hisar (1395/1396) and Rumeli Hisar (1452)' in *Acta Patristica et Byzantina*, 8 (1997) pp.144–49

Shaw, S. J., *The Financial and Administrative Organization and Development of Ottoman Egypt 1517–1798*, Princeton University Press, Princeton (1962)

Stein, M. L., *Guarding the Frontier: Ottoman Border Forts and Garrisons in Europe,* Tauris, London (2007)

Villain-Gandossi, C., 'Les Éléments Balkaniques dans la garnison de Trébizonde à la Fin du XVe siècle' in *Contributions à l'histoire économique et sociale de l'Empire ottoman*, Peeters, Leuven (1983) pp.127–47

GLOSSARY

Akçe	Silver coin.
Akritai	Army units guarding the Byzantine Empire's eastern border, facing the Muslim states of the Middle East.
Alatci	Craftsman or labourer.
Alaybey	Commander of a district of *timar* holders.
Anbarci	Storehouse keeper.
Avariz	Tax levied in wartime or for the construction of a fortress.
Beden	Crenellation.
Beylik	Small domain, independent or vassal of a greater state.
Cami	Mosque for congregational Friday prayers.
Cebeci	Armourer.
Cebehane	Armoury.
Derbendci	Guardians of roads and passes.
Gedik	Listing in a garrison or muster payroll.

Guruş	Large silver coin.
Hamam	Bath house including both hot and cold chambers.
Han	Inn, sometimes fortified.
Hisar	Fort or fortress.
Hisarli	Troops serving at a fort.
Kapu	Gate.
Kervansaray	Hostel on a major highway, sometimes fortified.
Kule	Tower.
Mescit	Small mosque or prayer room.
Meteris	Entrenchment or palisade.
Meydan	Open space, sometimes used for parades or training.
Mimar	Architect.
Mimarbaşi	Chief architect.
Miri anbar	Government storehouse.
Müstahfiz	Fortress soldier.
Müteferrika	Guards of a fortress commander, though also used more generally for fortress troops.
Namazgâh	Open-air mosque, often associated with a fortress or garrison base.
Ocak	Unit of Janissary infantry, deriving from military campfire; also a fireplace.
Oda	Room.
Palanka	Fortification made of earth-filled wooden palisades.
Saray	Palace.
Serhad	Frontier zone.
Siçan yol	Parallel trenches.
Tabiyye	Redoubt.
Vakfiye	Pious endowment, usually of money-raising property.

INDEX

References to illustrations are shown in **bold**.